TRAPPING 101

TRAPPING 101

A Complete Guide to
Taking Furbearing Animals

PHILIP P. MASSARO WITH PHILIP J. MASSARO

Skyhorse Publishing

Skyhorse Publishing books may be purchased in bulk at special discounts for sales promotion, corporate gifts, fund-raising, or educational purposes. Special editions can also be created to specifications. For details, contact the Special Sales Department, Skyhorse Publishing, 307 West 36th Street, 11th Floor, New York, NY 10018 or info@skyhorsepublishing.com.

Skyhorse® and Skyhorse Publishing® are registered trademarks of Skyhorse Publishing, Inc.®, a Delaware corporation.

Visit our website at www.skyhorsepublishing.com.

10 9 8 7 6 5 4

Library of Congress Cataloging-in-Publication Data is available on file.

Cover design by Tom Lau
Cover photos courtesy GettyImages; cover illustrations courtesy the author

Print ISBN: 978-1-5107-1633-9
Ebook ISBN: 978-1-5107-1634-6

Printed in China

This book is the product of the generosity of many people, who took the time out of their life to show a kid how to do things; the world would be a better place if more people were this generous.

Among those who taught me about trapping, certain names stick out, and I'd like to express my sincere gratitude, even though all these gentlemen have passed on. To David W. Miller, for showing me how to do just about anything, but especially about hunting and trapping. To Kingdom Proctor—my 4H leader—for handing a kid a bunch of used traps and inspiring a lifetime of adventure. To Harold Holsapple, the north country long-line professional trapper, for a plethora of insight and advice. To Harold (Pop) Ellis, for taking a young man coon hunting. And lastly, to my trapping partner Mike Drivas, with whom I spent so much time afield in the late 1970s and early 1980s.

—Philip J. Massaro, Linlithgo, New York, October 7, 2019

Table of Contents

Foreword

It goes without saying that I owe Phil Massaro a debt of gratitude for seeing my passion for trapping, my concern for the sport and its future, my commitment to family and tradition, and my utter respect for the animals . . . all animals.

Trapping was a sport that I was exposed to as a young boy, though I was removed from it for many years. Ironically, it was actually a writing career which brought me back into the trapping scene. I was on assignment, inking a story about a father-son duo who had been running a line together for over twenty years. That day, the fire inside of me was re-kindled, and it burned strong. Every fall since, I've spent more time overthinking a set or a specific crit-ter than anyone should. But, that's what trappers do. It's a chess match, and every single day you need to think about your next move. It's more than a game, though. It's an art, the original art. Without trap-ping, what would've pushed settlers west? I think about the mountain men and settlers every time I pull a beaver from a trap. I can only dream of trap-ping back then.

Phil and I share the love of history, but it's more than that for both of us. We spoke on the phone the other day, and talked about how trap-ping was a family "thing" for both of us. My uncle was the one who put steel in my hand, and showed me around the creeks and field edges. Phil's dad was the one who showed him the ropes. The days of trapping with my uncle are long-gone, but I've passed the sport on to my children, who have both done more in trapping than I had even dreamt about at their age. They run a winter weasel line each year, after the ermine have all turned white. They've both trapped several foxes, beavers, coy-otes, raccoons, and muskrats. My son, Tate, even has a bobcat under his belt. I hope that someday they have children of their own, and pass down the art of trapping. I hope that it spreads to their friends, like it has to my kids' friends. I hope they all stumble across this book, and find something in it that helps elevate their ability to outsmart a crit-ter on any given day.

We truly hope that you enjoy the book. It may have a title insinuating that it's a book for beginners, but there are enough small tricks of the trade and personal observations that we believe everyone will pick up something from its pages. Whether you're just looking to refine your coyote skills, or you want to learn how to begin a weasel line with your kids, the book has it all. Also included are stories of suc-cess and failure. If you're a seasoned trapper, you'll probably think there are parts of the book that are wrong, but like anything else in life, there are things to be learned no matter how experienced you may be. If you've been around trapping long enough, you'll surely think to yourself that you've been in our shoes. You might even crack a chuckle. If you're new to trapping, you might find pieces of the trapping scene that aren't for you. You might find it controversial. No matter how you view it, we hope that you find it informative.

Thank you for picking it up; I hope that you can't put it down. May the information in this book lead to as many happy trapping memories as I've had with my family.

—Matthew Breuer, outdoor author,
Bemidji, Minnesota

The authors, Philip J. Massaro and Philip P. Massaro.

Introduction

First and foremost, we'd like to welcome you to "Trapping 101." I say "we" because this book is a joint collaboration between yours truly—Philip P. Massaro—and my dear father, Ol' Grumpy Pants—Philip J. Massaro. You see, I was raised hunting, fishing, and trapping with my dad, and while he split his time between running hounds, deer hunting, and running a trap line all fall and winter,

The authors on safari in Tanzania.

I went on to become a big-game junkie. Now, that doesn't mean that I didn't enjoy trapping, but there are twenty-one years between us and the mid-1960s were not the mid-1980s. By the time I had a car, and the opportunity to run a trap line of my own, my father had established a land surveying business, and I began my apprenticeship to follow in his footsteps. However, for the previous two decades Grumpy Pants was obsessed with trapping, and I spent much of my youth helping him as best I could, and soaking up all the information I could.

Fast forward three decades to the present, and GP and I have been business partners in our land surveying business for fifteen years, and I have somehow found myself the author of five books on guns, ballistics, and hunting, as well as hundreds of magazine and Internet articles.

GP and I have been on safari together, and have hunted in the US and Canada together, but my second career has literally taken me around the world,

My brother Jamie with some raccoon hides, in the late 1970s.

having hunted four continents. Mind you, this is in no way a bragging session; it is an affirmation of my roots, as the farther I travel to hunt the remote places of the world, the more I appreciate those memories made with my father at home, at a young age, when we had little money.

At that time, the local world was as wild as anything I could've imagined, and to see my dad head off into the "wilds" with a basket full of steel, and then return with animals that a young man doesn't see every day, was downright magical. While my first job as assistant involved unrolling and fluffing frozen muskrat hides—seven-year-old fingers get cold very quickly—it quickly progressed to field trips, helping with the skinning, checking traps, and more. This is more than a trip down memory lane, though. This book came to fruition as a direct result of those years GP and I trapped together.

In my opinion, the ultimate result of hunting, trapping, or fishing is more than meat in the freezer, fur on the stretcher, or horns on the wall; it is the collection of memories. Those memories made with my father as a youth, as well as the process of putting his knowledge onto paper throughout the writing of this book, are filed away as some of my favorites.

I want you to understand—throughout the educational and informational sections of this book—that when you read the word "I," it will be referring to my father, as his knowledge and experience with trapping animals far eclipses mine.

He learned from experienced trappers old enough to be his father, guys who used the fur as a good part of their income each year, guys raised during the Great Depression and who knew how make do with little, and needed to use their heads to make things happen. Grumpy Pants absorbed that knowledge like a sponge as a young man just moved out of New York City, and built on this foundation through experimentation, discussion, and partnering with other trappers. He went on to be certified by the State of New York to teach trapper education—he and the other instructors gave me the course at ten years old—passing his knowledge to others, but that simply wasn't enough for my father.

I had sat down to dinner in Las Vegas with none other than Skyhorse's Jay Cassell—we were both attending the annual SHOT Show—when the topic of the Catskill Mountains came up. Jay had spent time there, and I explained how I had grown up in the shadows of those mountains. One thing led to another, and Jay indicated he needed a book on trapping; I excused myself from the dinner table, called my father, and set the deal up.

What you are about to read is my father's collection of experiences condensed into an instruction manual; you are, no doubt, going to become a better trapper as a result of his education. The majority of his experience is here in the Northeast, and predominately in the Hudson Valley, so you may have to adjust some of the ideas slightly for your particular environment. I do know, after listening to my father discuss trapping with colleagues from around the country, that the practices are so similar that the adjustments in technique are minimal.

If you've purchased this book, you're obviously interested in the art of trapping a furbearing mammal. I can think of no better teacher on the subject than my father. The art of outsmarting some of the wisest and wiliest animals nature has to offer requires diligence, dedication, and patience. I can pretty much guarantee that you're going to make some mistakes along the way—Lord knows I have—but the answers are within the covers of this book. Each step outlined is there for a reason, and having trapped with dad, I can tell you there is no cutting of corners, not if you want to be a successful trapper, consistently. So without any further ado, I present to you *Trapping 101*. I sincerely hope that trapping, and the people you meet and experiences you have as a result of the sport, make as many happy memories for you as it has for my father and me.

—Philip Massaro
Coxsackie, New York
July 12, 2019

Philip J. Massaro has been trapping since the mid-1960s.

Philip P. Massaro has been trapping with his father since the early 1980s.

Part 1

The History of Trapping— A Legacy of Exploration

Mankind has relied upon furs and skins for its survival, and durable clothing has invariably assisted in the survival of our species. As human beings migrated out of the tropical climates of eastern Africa and began to populate and explore the higher latitudes—where the weather was much less hospitable—fur played a very important role in our evolution and survival. The use of fur—along with bones, sinew, antlers, claws, and quite obviously meat—extended the life of humans and decreased infant mortality. It also allowed mankind to stay warm in an era when fire was utilized, though in a most inefficient manner, as the campfire isn't exactly a wood-burning stove, and a hide teepee doesn't have the greatest insulation value. Trapping—in one form or another—has been around almost as long as man has been on the earth. Native Americans used the pit trap, deadfalls, and snares, the Chinese documented the use of nets and pits in the fourth century B.C., and virtually every civilization can exhibit some example of the use of a trap in one form or another to procure meat, hides, or fur.

The fur trade across Europe was dominated by the Russian markets, which provided furs to the greater part of western Europe and Asia during the Middle Ages, which prompted the exploration of Siberia and its game-rich forests. Early on, the furs of beaver, wolf, and fox made up the bulk of the market, but as exploration pushed in the northern areas,

furs of sable, lynx, and Arctic fox were added to the lineup. By the 1500s, Europe had drastically overhunted and exploited her natural resources—including her population of furbearing mammals—and relied on importation and trade for their fur supply. Siberia was a major supplier, and the international value of fur made it a highly valuable commodity. Like our own country, the settling of Siberia can be directly tied to the pursuit of furbearers; many of those early outposts evolved into villages and cities that are thriving to this day.

The settling and westward expansion of our country in the sixteenth through nineteenth centuries can be directly tied to the natural resources this great land has to offer, and furbearing animals played a huge role in our history.

Here in North America, sailors on the island of Newfoundland were trading metal goods for beaver and otter pelts in the 1570s; one hundred years later, the Hudson's Bay Company was founded, by English Charter of King Charles II, in 1670. (As a note, the company exists to this day, as a chain

An old-time trapper.

of retail stores.) However, their primary business—from the time they were formed until commercial depression of the mid-nineteenth century—was the fur trade, and they were a dominating force in North American fur trapping. Hudson's Bay Company, at one point in time, owned what was known as Rupert's Land, which comprised the majority of middle Canada surrounding Hudson's Bay, as well as parts of Montana, the Dakotas, and Minnesota. The endeavor had proved itself worthy by procuring over £1,200 in fur in 1668–9, and exploration into the undiscovered valleys and mountain ranges of North America immediately commenced. Forts were established on the fringes, in order to fill the huge demand for fur, as beaver especially was in high demand. The soft under-fur of the beaver hide was prized by the millinery industry, and the beaver-felt hat was in vogue throughout Europe from the mid-1500s up until the mid-1800s, when it was replaced by the silk hat. The practice of felting beaver fur began when Europeans had traded for the well-worn beaver pelts of the Indians, and that wear exposed the thick, inner fur below the guard hairs. The inner fur could be easily sheared and felted for hat making; that fashion boom, which would last three centuries, was fueled primarily by American beaver pelts.

So plentiful were the furbearing mammals of the northern climes that men would risk life, limb, and the comforts of any semblance of civilization in order to trap in the wilds of an unsettled wilderness. Names like Jim Bridger, Jedidiah Smith, James Beckwourth, Jim Baker, Joseph Meek, Jean Baptiste Charbonneau, and William Henry Ashley bring to mind not only the great explorers and settlers of the American West, but tie in the importance of fur trapping to the westward expansion. Many of our major cities in the Midwest were founded as small trading outposts, with their primary reason for existence being the fur trade.

Early mountain men used the numerous rivers and streams as highways into the West, and as the population of beaver and other furbearers began to dwindle, they would push farther and farther into the unknown. Between 1825 and 1840, the mountain man Rendezvous was an annual event where all those adventurous souls would gather together, to sell their furs, resupply for the following season, share stories of the year's experiences, and perhaps pull a cork or two. These were a rough breed of men, risking life and limb in the cold rivers and streams, often spending months alone in a harsh wilderness, dealing with not only hostile Indians, but grizzly bears, mountain lions, and some of the worst weather possible.

Fur was so valuable that it became a monetary unit. Just as a dollar is called a "buck"—because a buckskin was equal in value to one dollar—fur was a medium of monetary value. The "made beaver" was Hudson's Bay Company's moniker for one male beaver pelt, itself a unit of monetary exchange, and eventually issued "made beaver" coins.

While the coins were only of value within the company and its employees, they eventually came in denominations of one beaver, one-half beaver, one-quarter beaver, and one-eighth beaver, and the system had an exchange rate to the British pound sterling. This allowed the frontier businessmen to trade with the indigenous peoples at a common rate, stabilizing the local economy. The made beaver coins came into common usage in the 1850s, when the number of actual available beaver pelts had seriously declined.

Hudson's Bay Company coins.

The first modern trap was the long spring leghold trap, put into production with uniform, replaceable parts by Mr. Sewell Newhouse, a blacksmith from Oneida County, New York in the early 1850s.

A lineup of Newhouse trap.

All the parts for a Newhouse trap were hand forged and rigorously inspected for flaws and uniformity. Being able to have parts of uniform dimension, interchangeable with other traps of the same size, was much appreciated by the trapping community, and by the end of the decade, Mr. Newhouse's traps were so popular that he would go on to sell hundreds of thousands of his traps. Even though the era of the fur boom on the frontier was over—at least for the huge beaver market—Newhouse would become a household name in the trapping industry. Prior to his standardization of the trap sizes and component dimensions, a leghold trap was a hand-forged affair, usually made to the best of the maker's ability, and from the best materials available, though it was difficult to repair or replace parts in the field.

The Oneida Iroquois would eventually leave New York, and as they were very friendly with Sewell Newhouse, they would play a role in spreading the word about the effectiveness of his trap design, as well

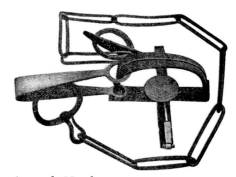

An early Newhouse trap.

as the quality of a Newhouse trap. Demand stayed high for Newhouse's traps, and the brand name and design thrives to this day.

Canadian inventor Frank Conibear made his mark on the trapping world by perfecting the body-gripping trap in the 1950s. Conibear's design takes the animal by the neck or body, either breaking the neck for an instantaneous kill, or grabbing them by the body and quickly suffocating the animal. Though there are many different brand names of body-gripping traps, they are all commonly referred to as Conibears. His invention would be accepted as one of the most humane ways to dispatch a furbearing animal; if set properly, a Conibear will kill even the largest beaver, and it became a favorite of trappers for nearly every animal other than fox, coyote, and wolves.

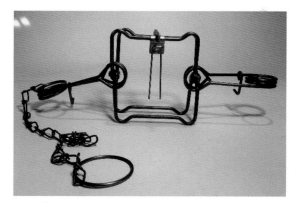

Frank Conibear's body-gripping trap.

Furs were not just used as luxury items for the rich, as they could be traded among the frontier people for firearms, knives, kettles, medicine, and other essentials. Though the greatest demand for fur was for the European hat trade, its value to mankind was clearly evident in the common usage of native furs in many of the indigenous tribes, a practice which remains to this day. I have used caribou fur mittens in Quebec when the temperatures dropped below -20°F. The Inuit and other Indians of the higher latitudes still rely on native furs; many musk ox hunters have been outfitted with the fur outerwear of their native guides, as it has proven to be warmer than any of the man-made synthetic gear. It's certainly a throwback to the time when natural fur was the best solution to surviving in the coldest of environments.

As the beaver-felt hat fell out of vogue, the nineteenth century demand for fur plummeted, and the era of the mountain man was over. However, the tradition of trapping fur was carried on by sportsmen across the nation. I was raised in a household where trapping was a staple; I watched my father—whose words will dominate this book—work a full-time job as a land surveyor, and run himself ragged running both coon hounds and a trap line. He and Mom started a family at a very young age, and though I was the oldest, I didn't realize until I got much older exactly how many Christmases and birthdays were paid for with the fur he had trapped or hunted. The exportation of fur to Russia in the late 1970s made for a very lucrative market during those years. I was only six or seven years old when it became my job to help stretch muskrat and raccoon hides (I wasn't allowed to touch the highly valuable red foxes and coyotes), and I clearly remember the long lines when the fur buyer used to come to Ralph's Gun Shop in Germantown, where a modern mountain man rendezvous would be held once a month or so. I also remember how proud I was of my father, when he'd bring in the best lot of fur. Other trappers would gather round, compare notes with Dad, and ask for advice; as a young kid it made me look at my father in the light that all little boys should: as a hero.

Trapping had been taught to him by those older sportsmen who rightfully took him under their wing—you see, my father was born in the concrete jungles of New York City and moved to rural upstate New York at ten years of age—where he learned how

The open places are constantly shrinking.

to hunt, fish, trap, and farm. That was handed to me as a youth, and had a huge influence on my love of the outdoors. However, by the mid-1980s, that Russian market dwindled, and we saw the decline of both trappers and houndsmen. Rabies became a real problem in the late 80s and early 90s, and the sight of rabid raccoons in the daylight, as well as rabid coyotes and foxes, was not uncommon. Farms began to be sold off and subdivided in our area—the Hudson Valley saw a boom in real estate, and the New York City transplants gobbled up many of the farms that were in their respective families for generations—and many of the hunting and trapping lands were now off limits. Yet, my father continued to trap; simply put, it is in his blood.

Though the conveniences of modern life have all but bred the instinct to trap, hunt, and fish out of society, there remain a good number of us who want to experience that older, more primitive way of life, and who aren't embarrassed to admit the blunt fact that all of our food was alive at one time. A good trapper, like a good hunter or angler, fully understands the circle of life, and becomes a steward of nature. The modern traps, lures, and accessories only aid in the common desire: to embrace our roots and enjoy the wild places that remain on God's green earth.

Let's not try to fool ourselves; we *Homo sapiens* are undeniably at the top of the food chain, and with that position comes a responsibility to properly utilize the natural resources of our planet. By studying the history of trapping we can gain several valuable lessons: how to properly utilize the population of furbearing animals, how to learn the habits of those animals, and (by not repeating the gluttonous over-harvesting of animals of past centuries) how to ensure that there will be animals left to trap for our grandchildren.

The world is shrinking, and as we humans continue to increase our population and encroach on the wild places, the available habitat for wildlife will inevitably shrink. The balance of nature is drastically affected by mankind, and the system of checks and balances must be implemented by man. The preservationist mentality has not worked out well, historically

speaking, and trapping has been an effective tool for as long as our recorded history will indicate. It is up to us to make the history of our time here, and as trappers we can make it a positive era.

Every time you boil your traps, or strap on a pack basket, you are undoubtedly touching history. You, as a trapper, are entrusted to carry on that history, to enjoy it yourself, and to pass it on to those younger than you in order to continue that history. Never again will we have the era of westward exploration, where we found an untamed land filled with game that was unfamiliar with man, yet the wild places that those who came before us had the wisdom to protect remain a haven for both the game and those who pursue it. There are a million excuses not to get your butt outdoors, especially in this modern world, but I promise you this: The memories and friends made while trapping in the woods and fields, forests and mountains, will be some of the most precious you'll have in your old age.

The Ethics of Trapping

The trapping of an animal has become quite the controversial topic in today's politically correct world; animal rights groups and their activists have damned the sport—along with hunting, fishing, and any other activity that doesn't meet their standards. Undoubtedly, the world has changed, yet the realities do not change with it, and I know that trapping can be a very useful tool for controlling pests and predators alike. However, in this modern era, we sportsmen and women need to police ourselves, and put our best foot forward.

Trapping, when performed by a diligent and responsible individual, is very effective. Responsibility is the key, as we are all under the microscope in the twenty-first century, what with social media and the generation of knee-jerk reactionaries. The last thing any respectable trapper wants is to cause undue suffering; it is our job to make sure that before the first trap is set, we have committed ourselves to being thorough, as well as dedicated. Leaving an animal in a trap because you're tired, preoccupied, or otherwise

The authors checking a dirt hole set from the road with the aid of binoculars. Checking traps frequently prevents undue suffering.

committed is no excuse; you need to be dedicated to checking your trap line twice a day, and if that isn't a possibility, spring or pull your traps.

Leaving an animal in a trap is not only unethical, but gives all the ammunition possible to the enemies of trapping, and puts us all in a very negative light. I liken trapping to being a dairy farmer; the cows don't understand when you're tired or sick, or about Christmas and birthday celebrations. Same goes for trapped animals, in that you simply owe it to the animal to quickly dispatch it or set it free.

I've seen trappers become over-eager with the size and/or length of their trap line, and biting off more than they could chew, with regard to available time. They would then struggle to check the traps in a timely fashion, and things would invariably fall apart. The size and number of sets in your trap line are directly correlative to the amount of time you have to responsibly handle them, and it's one of those instances in which you have to be completely honest with yourself.

Game laws need to be strictly adhered to, as do property rights. Getting caught trespassing isn't worth the prettiest fox, mink, or coyote, and if you obtain permission from a landowner to trap on his or her land, do everything in your power to make sure that landowner is happy to have had you on their property. Remember, your actions will influence the landowner's judgment of trappers, and will depend on whether or not future trappers will have a chance to participate in the sport. Our world is shrinking daily, and the room for pursuit of wild animals is shrinking with it. Therefore, access to private lands is becoming a commodity, and our behavior matters. A landowner doesn't want troubles, be it from a game warden investigating a violation, or having the neighbor's cat caught in a trap. So as a trapper, the best piece of advice I can offer is to be as honorable as possible, setting the example for other trappers, and helping to give trapping a good name.

Become proficient in releasing an animal from a trap (see the instructions in the Tips section of this book), so that the unwanted animals can survive unharmed. Avoid trapping in populated areas, where the possibility of catching house pets is a reality, and avoid making a set in a conspicuous area where passersby may see your animal in the trap before you have a chance to check it. This is not to say that we must hide or excuse the sport of trapping, but we should take steps to make the sport respectable, and any sort of laziness or disregard for the game laws or for the life of an animal will do nothing but further the agenda of those seeking to abolish trapping.

The bleeding hearts will proclaim the use of a leghold trap is cruel. Well, nature is cruel, life is cruel, and when we set out to understand the way nature works, those statements become quickly evident. A coyote can and will eat dozens of fawns each spring, just as skunks and raccoons will clean out a nest of turkey or grouse eggs in a heartbeat. Predators feed on the prey, and without some sort of control, the balance can easily be disturbed. An overabundance of predators can have a devastating effect on a good number of game species, and while hunting the predators can be an effective means of controlling the predator population, these are extremely smart and primarily nocturnal animals.

In addition, the condemnation of wearing fur has been a real issue in the last couple decades, though fur seems to be making a comeback as of late. Wearing an animal's skin has been an integral part of the survival of mankind, and just as we have a near-inexplicable attraction to both antlers and ivory, we have the same attraction to fur. There are those who feel terribly guilty about the killing of an animal for its fur, and while those same people will deem fur as a luxury or frivolity, it has historically made the difference between death and life for those in the extreme cold climes.

Ethically, we live in two worlds at once. We consider ourselves completely civilized, yet when the weather turns one way or another, or the electricity goes out, we return to primitive ways in a very short amount of time. Our civilized nature breaks down quickly, and things as simple as procuring a food source can become a challenge for those without the skills to handle a gun and a knife.

Trapping pits the wits of a human being against the superior senses of smell, sight, and hearing of the predator species, with we humans often coming out on the losing end of the equation.

The Public Image of Trapping

Our modern world is a topsy-turvy place; the recent wave of political correctness has all of us on eggshells, nearly apologizing for our own existence on the planet. While I believe this to be a bunch of hogwash, we outdoorsmen and women need to portray a positive public image. The animal rights activists— a fanatical, misinformed, and overzealous lot—are well organized, and will use any means necessary to put an end to hunting, fishing, and trapping. Their preservationist mentality is just silly; we humans have populated the majority of the planet, and the wildlife—from mice to elephants—has been forced to deal with that fact.

Trappers, much like hunters, need to be conservationists, as stewards of the land and its wildlife. You will see trapping referred to as barbaric, with the animal rights activists labeling you as cruel, selfish, ignorant, and many other adjectives that are not allowed to be printed in this book. Please understand that social media and the immediate access to Internet information puts us all under the microscope, and once an image is placed online, it is very difficult to remove it.

Advertisements showing skewed images of an animal suffering in a trap are a favorite of the ARAs, playing on the heartstrings of those people who rarely leave the comforts of their home, and have little idea how nature truly works. They choose to ignore the hard facts, not wishing to understand or even discuss the cruel effects of overpopulation and disease among the predators and target animals, let alone the effect that an overpopulation of predators and scavengers can have on the other species of wildlife. An overabundant population of skunks, raccoons, and opossums will wreak havoc on the nesting sites of the various game birds, just as an overabundant population of foxes, coyotes, bobcats, and fishers will decimate the deer fawns. These predators must be managed in order to give balance to the other species, and

King George III, adorned in fur.

whether or not a person is comfortable with the idea of using a trap to remove the surplus population of predators, it remains one of the most effective tools available.

You, the trapper, should hold your head high, yet behave in a manner that is respectable and an example for other trappers to follow. Again, this crazy world—all too often hypocritical—wishes to ignore the fact that were it not for hunting, trapping, and fishing, many of our ancestors would have perished in the wilds. In spite of what the politically correct faction would indicate, all of our food sources, including vegetables, were alive at one point in time, and in order to become food, that life had to be extinguished. Furbearing animals are a renewable resource, just as deer or evergreen trees are, and the brutal fact is that wonderful forests were cut down, the land tilled, and the wildlife driven off just to grow a crop of fruits or vegetables. Furbearing animals are as important as any other species, and whether we want to feel guilty about it or not, mankind is the dominant species on the planet. Sitting in the comfort of your home, staying warm by burning oil or using the products of a coal-burning electric plant, and eating the food necessary to sustain you—having a farmer or butcher do your dirty work for you—while proclaiming that the outdoorsman, whether a hunter, trapper, or fisherman, is a barbarian from an ignorant age is completely hypocritical.

In fact, the complete opposite way of thinking is closer to the truth. Farmed fur, poultry, and livestock leads a much poorer life than does a wild animal, and—apparently unbeknownst to the animal rights activists—no hunter, trapper, or fisherman wants to take the last of any species he or she pursues. Simply put, the true sportsman does more to propagate the species they are pursuing than anyone else. Our license fees pay to preserve lands, giving the wildlife room to live, and us the opportunity to enjoy the bounty of the land as our forefathers did, and there is absolutely nothing wrong with that.

Those fanatics who choose to become aggressive and confrontational with a sportsman or with those who choose to wear fur must be dealt with carefully. I would recommend joining an organization that has access to legal representation that is experienced in the legalities and prosecution of those fanatics who choose to take matters in their own hands. Many states have passed legislation which protects the sportsman from harassment, and I wish that the Federal Government would follow suit, passing a blanket law which allows the ethical, law-abiding sportsman to pursue his or her passion unmolested. Remember, in these volatile times, the positive image of the outdoorsman is more crucial than ever, and it is ultimately up to us to portray that image.

I have noticed that the wearing of fur garments—coats, vests, muffs, and fur-trimmed clothing—has become fashionable once again, with many designers of fashion wear embracing real fur. Though the topic remains a hot bed for argument, mankind has always embraced fur, either as a necessity or a luxury. Members of the radical animal rights groups like PETA and Animal Liberation Front have, in the past, gone so far as throw paint on people wearing a fur coat, and one fashion designer had a radical activist put a dead raccoon on her plate while dining at a prominent restaurant. This type of behavior is not only illegal, but immoral. To combat this effect, I believe that we outdoorsmen and women need to band together, and joining the membership of one of the major organizations is an effective means of doing just that. The National Trappers Association and Fur Takers of America are just two examples of well-organized outfits that fight for our rights as sportsmen, and the cost of a membership to one of these groups is a worthy investment. Just as it is in the hunting world, no organization is perfect, but the collective is much more powerful than the individual.

Education has proven to be an effective tool, and will continue to be the best means we have to sway the public opinion. Don't be afraid to properly educate yourself, so when someone asks about the sport of trapping, you can intelligently answer questions, in order to show the benefits of the sport. Take a kid trapping; as a hunter, shooter, trapper, and outdoorsman, I feel I have a personal obligation to share the wisdom I've gathered, and hand that down to a youngster just as it was handed down to me.

Each year, the antis try to get legislation passed to diminish or abolish the rights of trappers; in 2017, for example, Montana voted on I-177, a ban on trapping. The antis insist that the "majority of Montanans oppose trapping," yet the vote showed that by a margin of almost two to one, Montanans support trapping, and sportsmen alike. However, without the constant support of the various organizations—the Montana Trappers Association came out strong for this one—sooner or later the antis will gain a foothold, and once they do it is awfully difficult to undo it.

Only we can combat the misnomer of "barbarism" associated with trapping; we need to do everything in our power to ensure that traps are checked at least once daily, in order to dispatch and collect or release trapped animals to minimize any undue suffering. All animals die, that is a fact of life, but as fur was shunned by the bleeding hearts, both mange and rabies became a serious issue. To watch an animal die that slow, painful, agonizing death is a terrible experience, but one that the animal rights activists generally refuse to concern themselves with, as it isn't visible from the comforts of their home. These diseases can be transmitted quickly to domestic livestock and household alike, not to mention the legitimate threat of transmission to humans. Rabid raccoons, foxes, and coyotes have been known to end the life of our beloved pets, as well as biting children. At that stage, many who are opposed to trapping will throw their hands in the air, asking why no one has done something about this problem.

Here in upstate New York, a black bear took an infant off the deck of a house, killing the baby. Population control—in this instance by hunting—might have saved the life of that baby. Though this may be an extreme example, many people are forced to go through the long and painful process of shots required to combat rabies each year, as a result of overpopulation of predators. To reiterate, the sportsman's goal is not the eradication of any species, but the healthy balance of nature, and the sensible utilization of the renewable resources.

Part 2

Traps and Gear

To start the trapping of animals, you will need a set of specific traps and gear, as well as the supporting equipment. Modern traps come in many different shapes and sizes, having specific uses and applications, with quite a bit of overlap. You certainly don't need to own every size of each trap style, but you will need some variety, depending on which animals you plan to trap, and what your natural surroundings are. Herein, we will discuss the different styles, sizes, and nomenclature of the wide variety of traps, their applications for varying species, as well as the assorted supporting gear needed to be a proficient trapper.

Traps

The modern leghold trap is a direct descendant of the ancient wood and sinew traps. The basic concept,

An early bear trap.

throughout history, is to use stored energy to quickly close the trap jaws once a trigger has been activated. Our modern leghold, as well as body-gripping traps, use a steel spring for the source of stored energy; steel is a durable material, and will give nearly a lifetime of use if properly cared for. The means of delivering that stored energy varies with each trap design, but from the smallest mouse traps to the largest bear traps, a spring is a very effective means of delivering stored energy.

Basic Nomenclature

Understanding the basic nomenclature of a trap and being able to identify the various parts is important; while learning the various techniques outlined in this book, as well as when discussing the sport with other trappers, a good understanding of the parts of a trap is paramount to the best field performance. A good tip handed down from a veteran trapper may seem confusing unless you are familiar with the terms he or she is using to describe a set and or trap application.

All traps will have a trigger, though they vary from design to design. The common leghold traps—the coil spring and long spring—will use a combination of a dog and a pan, while the body-gripping traps—such as the famous Conibear trap—will have a wire trigger and top latch. When either type of trigger is activated, it releases the stored energy in the springs, which are under tension when the trap is set. The springs may be a piece of coiled steel—for the coil spring trap design—or a piece of steel bent in the shape of a "V" or "U," which is compressed to store energy, in the long spring designs. Depending on the design, the spring may directly act on the trap jaws, in the case of the long spring traps, jump traps, and body-gripping traps, or use a spring lever to close the jaws, in the case of a coil spring trap.

The trap jaws do the majority of the work; they are responsible for holding the animal by foot, neck, or body, once the trap has been triggered or sprung. The common "standard" trap jaws are a simple piece of square-edged steel which meet when closed; they are curved or bow shaped in the long spring, jump, and coil spring traps, or straight in the case of body-gripping traps.

Refinements have been made in trap jaw design, including the offset jaws (designed to avoid broken bones, and allow blood flow to the trapped foot, should you decide to release the animal from the trap), and the "soft catch" jaws, which utilize a rubber-type material on the inside of the jaws to minimize damage to the animal's foot. The double jaw design has an additional piece of metal affixed to the underside of the standard jaw design, giving an additional bearing surface to the trap, and prevents "chew-offs," where an animal will chew its own foot off to get out of the trap. This design denies the animal access to that part of its foot that is in the trap. For body-gripping traps, the jaws are a simple piece of round steel, as the trap is designed to use a scissor action to hold the animal by the body or neck; the goal being to kill the animal upon the springing of the trap. The body gripping trap is an unforgiving design. The dog-proof coon trap uses a round piece of heavy-gauge steel wire, inside the tube, and uses the spring tension to keep the coon's foot and leg inside the cylindrical metal tube.

Dealing with long spring traps and coil spring traps, you'll find many similar features, with the exception of the spring design. Both are constructed with a bottom piece or base, and cross, to which are attached the jaw posts, pan post, and dog. The shank of the pan will be attached to the pan post, and built with a notch at the top of the pan shank. The dog will be placed under the notch, and this combination holds the jaws open, until disturbed when an animal steps on the pan. At this point in time, the energy stored in the springs is released, and the jaws quickly shut.

A body-gripping trap will have a latch on one jaw—shaped roughly like a key—with multiple half-moon notches, for varying degrees of jaw space. On the opposite jaw, a swinging trigger, with two protruding wires, swivels in a pendulum motion—in either direction—to push the latch off of this trigger jaw, allowing the trap to close.

All of these traps will have some sort of attachment point, used to affix a swivel and chain to the trap. This chain will anchor the trap to a stationary object or drown wire, to prevent an animal from running off with the entire trap.

Types of Traps

There are many different types and styles, each having their specific advantages, applications, and drawbacks. I will attempt to familiarize you with each type, its general applications, sizes in which they are currently available, and their advantages and disadvantages. Let's break down the different types by their construction.

The Long Spring

The aptly named long spring is probably the oldest style of leghold trap in use today, using one or two long metal springs to close the trap jaws. There are many different manufacturers, sizes, and applications for the long spring trap. Long spring traps are divided into two groups: single long spring and double long spring. The single long spring traps are generally reserved for trapping weasels, minks, and muskrats, while the double long spring traps are used for larger animals such as raccoons, woodchucks, foxes, coyotes, bobcats, lynx, mountain lions, and wolves.

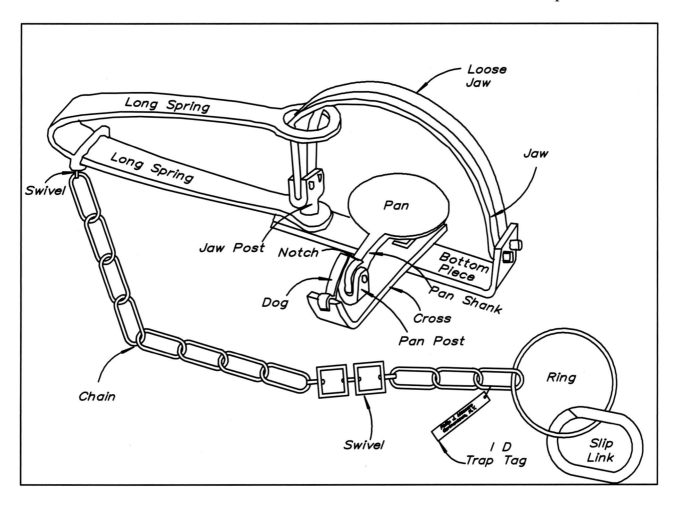

Single Long Spring Traps

These traps are currently available in size #0 and #1—though I have older single long-spring traps from Victor in size #1½ and #2—and have the advantage of being heavier than their coil spring counterparts. This weight advantage aids in the quick dispatch of minks and other animals in water drown sets, as the heavier trap helps to drown the animal. The single long spring traps are also easier and faster to set, helping to maximize your time on your trap line. The single long spring trap was my personal choice when trapping minks and muskrats, where I predominately used a drown set for these animals. The size #0—with its 3½-inch jaw spread—is perfect for muskrats and minks alike, especially when space is limited, and a smaller trap will fit the situation better. The larger #1—having a four-inch opening between the jaws—can be a more effective trap, if space permits; I like the additional weight and strength for most applications, if I have the room.

The single long spring trap currently comes in three styles: standard, double-jaw (which will prevent an animal from chewing its toes off, and pulling out of the trap), and "stop loss," which features an extra spring-loaded bail, to keep the animal's head from reaching its wrist to chew it off. I have only seen the "stop loss" feature available in size #1 single long spring.

The single long spring has its disadvantages as well; though the single long spring trap's additional weight definitely helps in a drown set, that weight will be cumbersome in your trap basket, as well as taking up additional precious space. The single long spring trap is more expensive than its coil spring counterpart—by about 10 percent, depending on where you shop.

Double Long Spring Traps

This design is similar to the single long spring, but has an extra spring on the opposite side of the trap jaw hinge. They are available in sizes #11 (simply a #1, with an extra spring), #2, #3, #4, #4½, #5, and #5 with teeth, for wolves and mountain lions. Please check your local trapping laws to make sure traps with teeth are legal to use; many states have made their use illegal. This variety of different sizes makes the double long spring trap a very versatile design, yet like the single long spring, these traps are heavy and bulky. The double long spring trap can be used for virtually any animal, up to and including wolves and bears. As a note, all of the modern bear traps—and some are huge, with a jaw spread of seventeen inches, weighing forty-eight pounds, and having a total end-to-end spread of almost four feet!—are double long spring traps.

Double long spring traps come in standard jaw configuration, double jaw, and offset jaws. The most popular double long spring traps are sizes #2 and #3, as these are a perfect choice for raccoons, foxes, and coyotes, some of our most popular furbearers.

Some single and double long spring traps will feature a nut and brass washer on the connection between the trap pan and frame, in order to eliminate any pan wobble, as well as allowing the trapper to set the pan tension. I much prefer this design over the traditional stamped steel connection between pan shank and trap frame. Were I buying new long spring traps, I would ensure that they had the bolt/nut/washer attachment to give me more control over pan movement and tension.

The double long spring trap.

The coil spring traps.

The Coil Spring Leghold Traps

The coil spring leghold trap is a compact design—in comparison to the long spring traps—and relies on the energy of the compact set of coil springs to deliver its energy. There are many different manufacturers, sizes, and applications for the coil spring trap. Coil spring traps are divided into two groups: double coil spring and four-coiled coil spring. The double coil spring traps are generally reserved for trapping lighter animals like minks, raccoons, foxes, coyotes, skunks, woodchucks, opossums, and muskrats, while the four-coiled coil spring traps are used for larger animals such as Eastern coyotes, wolves, and beavers. Due to their popularity, there are more coil spring traps on the market than any other design; most trapping supply stores will carry more assortments of coil spring traps than their long spring counterparts. I also find the coil spring traps easier to conceal when land trapping.

Double Coil Spring Traps

These lighter, handy traps are available in size #1, #1½, #1.65, #1¾, #2, and #3. Generally speaking, in my opinion, the double coil spring traps are faster than their long spring counterparts. I believe this to be a result of a higher spring tension and resulting energy transfer. The smallest double coil spring traps—the #1—is perfect for minks and muskrats, while the slightly larger #1.65, #1½, #1¾, and #2 are ideal for raccoons and foxes, with the #2 being the smallest double coil spring trap I'd recommend for coyotes. The #2 double coil spring, with its jaw spread of 5½ inches, is also a perfect bobcat trap.

The compact nature of the double coil spring trap makes it much more versatile; it is the most common trap used today. I prefer them for their price, size, and weight, and ability to be tuned and repaired. This design allows the owner to replace springs and other parts in comparison to the long spring traps.

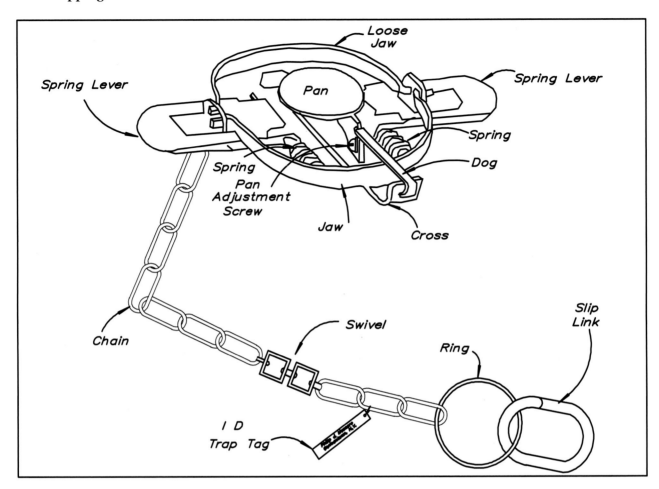

Four-Coiled Coil Spring Traps

These traps have the same configuration as the double coil spring traps, but simply have an extra set of springs in order to make the trap stronger, faster, and more resistant to "pull outs." The larger trap

Four-coiled coil spring trap.

sizes—such as the #3, #4, #5, and the huge #9—are all available in four coiled configuration, as well as the smaller sizes such as #1½, #1¾, and #2. Note that the smaller sized traps have a smaller set of extra springs in comparison to the larger #3 and up.

I prefer the larger, four-coiled traps for stronger animals like badgers, wolverines, coyotes, mountain lions, and wolves. The smaller varieties are useful for raccoons—for example, I find a #1½ four-coiled trap comparable to a #1¾ or #2 double coil—as they are very strong for their size, not to mention crafty.

Comparing the Two

I generally prefer the double coil spring traps for their affordability, ease of setting, and for trapping under ideal conditions, as well as for the "lighter" animals. I lean upon the four-coiled traps when conditions are not ideal, such as freezing temperatures or wet, heavy soil, or when the possibility of attracting a larger, heavier animal may exist. For example, a fox set that could be visited by a large male coyote would be better served by a four-coiled trap than a standard double coil spring trap. The four-coiled traps are more expensive, but will show their value when you have an animal in the trap, as opposed to a sprung trap and lost animal.

Jump Traps

A jump trap uses a single leaf-type spring, hinged at one corner of the trap frame.

A No. 1 Oneida jump trap.

When the trap is triggered, the spring is released, and as the spring frame surrounds the jaws of the trap, those jaws are quickly closed. These traps are becoming a rarity these days (as I believe they are out of production), though they can be effective for the various water/drown sets. I feel that the double coil spring traps are a better choice for dirt hole sets and other land trapping scenarios, as the jump traps are equipped with just one spring lever versus two for the double coil spring trap. Today's jump traps—when available—are offered in size #1, #3, #4, and #14 (which is a factory-made #4 trap, but with teeth, common among beaver trappers).

Here is a list of the common trap sizes and their approximate jaw spread.

Size—Jaw Spread
#0–3½"
#1–4"
#1½–5"
#1¾–5-⅜"

#1.65–5-⁷⁄₁₆"
#2–5-½"
#3–5-¾"
#4–6-¼"
#5–7-¼"
#9–9-⅛"
#14–6-¼" with teeth

Body-Gripping Traps (Conibear)

The body-gripping trap was perfected and made popular by Canadian inventor Frank Conibear in the 1950s, and works just as intended.

The #220 Conibear trap.

When properly set, a Conibear trap will break an animal's neck, killing it quickly and humanely. These traps make an excellent choice for aquatic settings, such as the sets for beavers, muskrats, and minks, though they can easily serve on dry land when trapping raccoons, skunks, and opossums. The body-gripping traps are not intended for foxes, coyotes, or wolves.

The term "Conibear"—while actually a brand name—has become synonymous with any body-gripping trap, and as you read and discuss trapping, you will hear the two terms used interchangeably. When I refer to a Conibear trap throughout this book, please interpret that as any of the various brands of body-gripping traps.

There are two styles of this trap: square and round, with the square variety being much more popular than the round variety. Both styles are available in single spring and double spring configuration. The rectangular, single spring Conibears are available in sizes #110, #150, #159, #50, and #60,

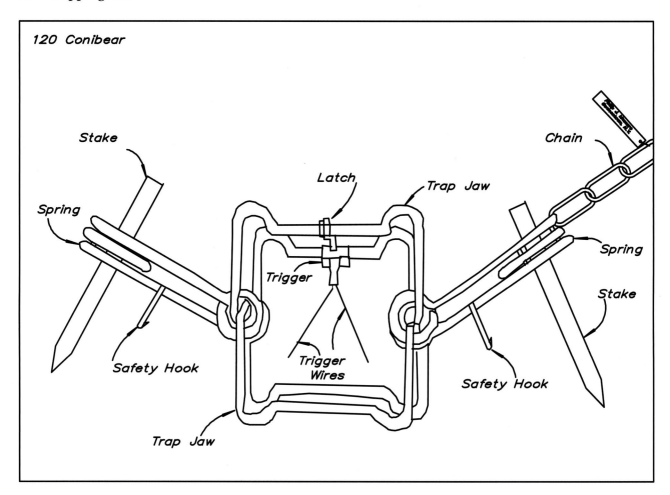

120 Conibear

Stake

Chain

Latch

Trap Jaw

Spring

Spring

Trigger

Stake

Safety Hook

Trigger Wires

Safety Hook

Trap Jaw

while the rectangular double spring Conibears are available in sizes #120, #155, #160, #220, #280, and #330 (the last being an excellent trap for beaver). The circular single spring traps are available in sizes #40, #50, and #110, with the circular double spring traps come in sizes #160, #220, #330, and #440.

Cage Traps (Also Known as Live Traps)

These are traps which do not hold any particular part of an animal's body, but rather use a cage and a door or doors to trap the animal, allowing it to move freely within the cage, unharmed. The trigger mechanism is usually a see-saw type plate where bait is placed, and when this plate is disturbed, it releases the latches holding the doors open, allowing them to close and lock. They are particularly useful when trapping in urbanized or semi-urban environments, where the possibility of a domestic animal coming into the trap site is a reality. Should you need

to release someone's pet, or relocate a nuisance animal without having to take its life, the live trap is an excellent method. Havahart is one of the most popular brands of live cage traps, and much like Conibear, the name Havahart has become synonymous with the cage traps.

The cage traps (generally) come in two styles: two-door and one-door, indicating the amount of entrances/exits in the design. The one-door traps come in a variety of sizes, labeled differently by each manufacturer, but run as such: 5"x5"x16," 7"x7"x17," 9"x9"x24," 10.5"x12"x32" (a good choice for raccoon), 12"x12"x29," 12.5"x14.5"x36," and 15"x15"x42" (perfect for bobcat). The two-door variety come in the following sizes: 5.75"x7.25"x17.5," 7"x7"x24," 11"x13"x42," and 12.5"x14.5"x36.5."

I tend to prefer the two-door models because of their appearance to the animal; animals will (in my experience) enter a tunnel—which is what the two-door cage trap will appear to be—easier than a dead

A two-door live trap, from Havahart.

end enclosure. The one-door models will make wary animals more hesitant to enter the trap and investigate the bait source, but the two-door models can easily be camouflaged to appear tunnel-like.

A live trap should be anchored like any other trap, and I like to place a heavy stone or two on top of the trap to keep the trap stabilized; the place you will set the trap will not always be the ideal, uniform level ground. Placing a stone on the top will also prevent the live trap from moving once the animal has first entered the trap; if the trap were to move, you risk the chance of having the animal back out of the trap.

The live trap can also be used to drown furbearers, by totally submerging the trap completely in water. This technique can work for skunks, opossums, raccoons, and minks, without damaging the pelts at all.

Dog-Proof Coon Traps

The (almost) "dog-proof coon trap" is relatively new to the trapping world as compared to Conibear and especially the leghold trap.

It is named for the design; the small cylinder used as a body for this trap prevents a common dog from getting its paw caught in the trap. They are all based on the same principle; they have a cylindrical or rectangular body about four to five inches long, with about a 1¼-inch opening at the top, standing almost vertical. At the top there is a spring-loaded heavy wire bail; when triggered it will catch and hold anything that is in the inside of the body. The release mechanism is located on the inside and at the bottom of the body. There are two types of release mechanisms. One will only fire when the trigger is pulled upward; the other type fires when the trigger is pulled

The dog-proof coon trap.

upward *or* pushed downward. The theory is when the inside of the body is filled with bait, a raccoon will put its agile front paws down inside the body of the trap to take out the bait, and the downward pressure or its upward pressure on the bait and trigger will set off the trap.

Gear

The following is a list of supportive equipment that a trapper will use while trapping. The list contains items you personally might not need, because not every trapper sets out to trap every animal in every habitat. This list will also give you the ability to understand when the terms are used to instantly know what the items are used for, and get a mental picture of them when you are reading instructions about different sets.

Trap Stakes

Simple stake, made from hardwood or metal.

They are attached to the end of your trap chain and their prime function is to hold the trap in place, even with a captured animal pulling on it. I personally only use iron or steel trap stakes, usually fashioned from reinforcing rod with some sort of cap or nut welded to one end, and sharpened at the other.

A trap stake made from reinforcing rod.

Trap Anchors

Trap anchors are a method of affixing your trap to the set when stakes are impractical, or you just would like to use anchors. There are many different styles to choose from. You can make them yourself, but I strongly advise purchasing them in the beginning. They are small blade-like pieces of metal with a cable attached, that are driven into the ground with a special rod to a satisfactory depth. When pulled upward, they turn right angles to the ground, making them almost impossible to pull out. They work very well, and are much lighter than traditional trap stakes.

Grapples

Grapples are used in place of stakes and anchors, mostly when soil conditions are such that a stake or anchor will not hold.

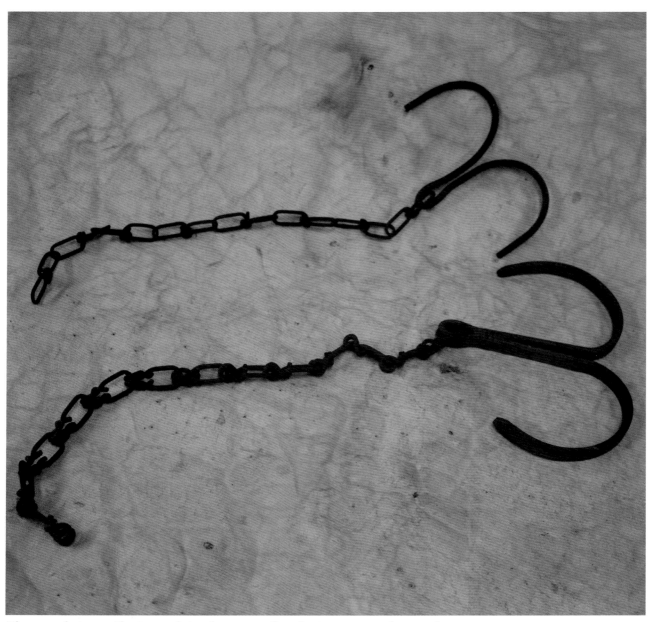

The grapple is an effective and simple means of anchoring a trapped animal.

They are also used when you do not want your catch to be seen at or near the set, and when trapping in snow. The use of a grapple always involves the use of a longer chain to make it much more functional. It is a two- or three-prong hook-like device, which when dragged along the ground becomes entangled with the first piece of vegetation, fence, or fallen tree limbs it encounters. The advantage of a grapple is that it eliminates the work of using a stake or anchor, especially when the ground is frozen. The disadvantage is that you have to look for or track up the trapped animal, and without snow cover this can take some time. I have in my possession a three prong fox grapple given to me in the 1960s, that had been made in the late nineteenth century. It belonged to the grandfather of the gentleman who gave it to me. Grapples are available from most trapping supply houses, but you can make them easily yourself. I would suggest purchasing a few different types first and then attempt to make the type you think is the best for you.

Trap Chains

This is not only the chain that comes with the trap, but also any additional chain you may need to add to the original chain to make it longer.

As a general rule, all trap chains should have a swivel at each end and one in the middle. When using grapples you will definitely need extra lengths of chain. Again, do not forget the swivels.

Trap Wire

Trap wire is wire used not only to connect traps, but for numerous other tasks. The gauge of wire is very important; I would use a gauge no thinner than #10.

Trap Swivel

The trap swivel is a simple device that prevents the trap chain from becoming twisted and bound.

The elongated chain on this Herter's trap has a homemade swivel in the middle.

The trap swivel will prevent an animal from getting a mechanical advantage on the trap.

Once trapped, an animal tends to work in a circle, and if the chain becomes bound, it allows the animal to apply more force and free itself from the trap. All trap chains should have at least three swivels, one at each end and one in the middle. I used to make them myself out of very short sections of one-inch pipe and common nails, but I have found that commercial ones are better and save a lot of time.

Slip Link

This is a link that will quickly attach to the end of your trap chain and attaches to the trap stake; it allows the trap chain to move freely around the metal stake.

Pan Covers

Pan covers are rather self-explanatory; they are covers over trap pans, which will prevent the dirt sifted over your trap from collapsing and settling in under the trap pan. That sifted dirt can prevent the pan from moving downward, thus not allowing the trap to fire. Pan covers are sold commercially and made from different materials.

A pan cover can be as simple as a large basswood leaf to commercial manufactured covers made from durable material. A short list of materials used for pan covers is: wax paper, boiled and dyed canvas, window screen (nylon and aluminum), and fiberglass. I personally prefer the canvas type. I make them myself out of material (cotton duck) from my worn-out, ten-ounce Carhartt pants. I cut them out to a perfect size to fit my different trap sizes, cut a slot for the trap dog, and throw them in the barrel when dying my traps. Let them air dry and store them in clean freezer bags for future use.

A wax paper pan cover.

Pan Blockers

A pan blocker is a light, fluffy, water-resistant material, placed under the pan, used to prevent any material from filling in under the pan and preventing the trap from firing. Material can range from washed, clean sheep's wool to polyester stuffing from a new pillow.

Trap Tag

Trap tags are tags with your name and address printed on them. In most states it is mandatory to have a tag on every trap.

Trap tags are usually placed on the trap chain. I use the copper tags, attach them to the trap chain, and wrap them around the chain. This keeps them safe when the animal fights to get free, and not in the way when making the set.

Drop Cloth

This is a cloth or tarp used to kneel on while making

One of Dad's trap tags from the 1970s.

a dirt set. Its purpose is to prevent the transmission of human and foreign odors onto the set. I use a rubber sheet, about three feet square. I mark one side, so I always know to put the same side down facing the ground, and when folding it up I fold the ground side in to keep it odor free. A rubber sheet can be washed easily and will not absorb foreign odors as readily as canvas.

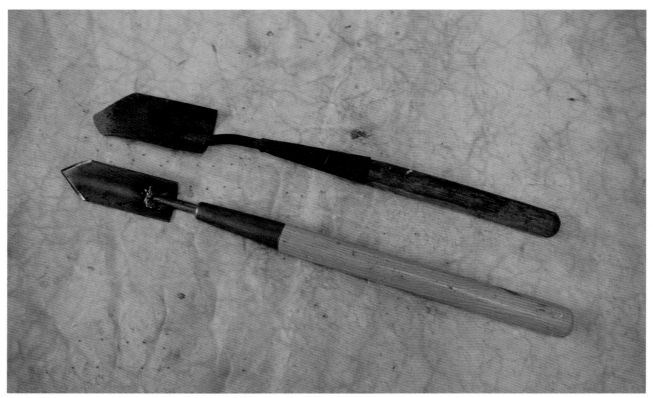

Long-handled trap trowels of varying widths.

Trowel

Trowels come in a wide variety of sizes and blade or spade designs, from handheld models to long handle ones.

You should have both a handheld model (a garden trowel) and a long-handle model, with a handle of about twenty to twenty-four inches long. Trowels are used to dig your bait holes and pockets, dig out your trap beds, and for stunning and dispatching trapped animals by giving them a quick blow with the flat side of the spade part of the trowel on top of the head.

Hoe

This tool is for the most part a regular garden hoe, but with a twenty-two-inch handle.

I found a very well-made hoe with a broken handle, which I replaced and cut down to twenty-two inches. Ideally, the blade should only be between three to four inches wide. Try to keep the blade fairly sharp, as it also comes in handy for cutting sod and weeds around your sets. Hoes made especially for trappers are available from trapping supply stores.

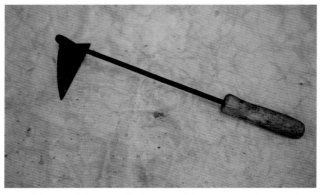

One form of the simple hoe, which can dig dirt, and cut roots and sod.

Sifters

Looking like a baking pan with a wire grate for the bottom, a sifter is used primarily to sift out non-wanted material when covering a trap.

It can also be used to shred and distribute dry grass on your sets, so they blend in to the natural surroundings. I also use it to replace snow when needed at snow sets. They come in different sizes and are made up of different materials. I use an all metal one, about eight by ten inches. I like it best because I can just throw it in the trap dying tub to clean it and be

The author's well-worn sifter.

sure it is odor free. Also, it is much more durable then the type made of wood and screen. There have been times where one a little larger than the one I currently use would have come in handy.

Pick Hammer

This is a combination tool: On one end is a hammer head, for driving stakes, and on the other end is a dull, wide, chisel-like end. The chiseled end is invaluable for chopping out trap beds, especially when the ground is frozen.

Bait Fork

Used to place bait at your set. I use a US Army mess kit fork, but any large fork will work.

Pack Basket

Pack baskets come in many sizes and are made of different materials. The most common or traditional ones are made of hardwood, followed by the ones

made of fiberglass. Both have their advantages and disadvantages.

The hardwood baskets are lighter and better ventilated. An array of pouches can be attached to the perimeter at the top to hold your lures, baits, and urines. The disadvantages of the hardwood baskets are that they are more difficult to wash and may become broken in spots if dropped on a rock. They must also be coated with polyurethane to prolong their resistance to the elements. Though more durable, the disadvantages of the fiberglass baskets is that they are that they are noisy and a little uncomfortable on your back. I find that they will slide easily on snow if not set down perfectly upright. The advantages are that you can readily hose them out when they need a cleaning, and most come with a separate outside compartment for your baits, lures, and urines. Most trappers end up with two containers when running their trap line: a container for long overland treks (usually a pack basket with shoulder straps) and a

The author's hardwood trapping basket.

The author's pack basket in the field.

plastic bucket when working close to their mode of transportation.

As to size, a hardwood basket about twenty inches high, with a fourteen-inch opening at the top, tapering down to about ten inches at the bottom, is a good working size. Size all depends on the amount of equipment you intend to carry and the distance you intend to carry it.

Spray Bottle

These are used primarily for applying urine to the set, and having a good number on hand is a sound idea.

Boston Round Glass Bottles

These are small bottles that lures and other trapping liquids are kept in for use on the trap line.

Trap Wax

This is the wax used to coat clean and dyed traps.

Dyed trap wax.

Spray bottle and various lures.

This waxing process not only keeps them from rusting, but speeds up trap function as well. There are many types of trap wax available. I personally use 100 percent pure bleached bee's wax, as I have found this wax works the best for me.

Trap Dye

This is used to coat your traps to a uniform dark color and also give them a temporary rust-resistant coating. You can buy commercial trap dye or you can use ingredients found in nature to dye your traps. In this book we give you detailed instructions for using natural materials to dye your traps.

Gloves

This is one trapping item for which you should never let cost dictate which style you purchase. For land trapping, a pair of rubber or neoprene coated, insulated gloves are a must.

If you intend to trap swamps and streams, a pair of shoulder-length, insulated gauntlets is also necessary. For trapping foxes and coyotes, the gloves should be of a length to come up at least midway between your wrist and your elbow. These gloves should only be worn when preparing your sets. Never wear them when applying bait or lure; but the application of urine is okay. Place them in a large freezer bag when not in use. In addition to those gloves you'll need to wear while making your sets, purchase a good pair of winter gloves, well lined to keep your hands warm when the weather turns cold. Cold hands do not work well!

Boots

When putting out and running a trap line, the wearing of rubber footwear is almost a given; when it comes to foxes and coyotes, it is a must. Even if you do not intend to trap foxes or coyotes, you will usually encounter water in one form or another on a normal trap line. If you are going to trap foxes,

A good pair of thick rubber gloves is very important.

coyotes, or muskrats, I strongly suggest you invest in a pair of rubber hip boots, and if you intend to trap in cold weather, get an insulated pair. If you intend to trap beavers, I would purchase a pair of chest waders. When trapping foxes and coyotes, hip boots can eliminate the need for a drop cloth when kneeling at the set. They can be washed off at every stream crossing, along with your rubber-coated gloves. Store them in an odorless place, out of direct sunlight and extreme heat (the ultraviolet rays will deteriorate the rubber). Always hang them by their heels. If the hip boots have been hanging for a long period of time, always check the inside of them for biting insects such as spiders, bees, scorpions, and the like; I'm talking from experience.

Claw

This is a simple three-pronged garden tool that is available most everywhere garden tools are sold. It is used for scraping out sod and making marks to imitate an animal's activity while digging.

Small Whisk Broom

This is a small handheld broom, used to level out the soil at dirt holes, flat sets, and any set where a trap is buried. It also comes in handy to blend in sets with surrounding material or snow.

Hatchet

A small hatchet always comes in handy; whether it is driving trap stakes, cutting a tree limb for a drag, cutting up a piece of a large bait, or chopping frozen ground for a trap bed. Find a durable and comfortable hatchet, and you'll have a friend for life.

Pliers or Vice Grips

You'll need one or the other, though I prefer vice grips because you can use them *most* of the time as a pair of pliers and they also make removing a trap stake much easier, by twisting the stake left and right while pulling up.

Screwdriver

Should always have one handy. I prefer a multi-tool,

which I can wear on my hip and which has a variety of tools all in one, both types of screwdrivers among them. I also like a Swiss Army knife.

Knives

A trapper needs to have a few different varieties of knives. You'll need one type for general purposes, like a pocketknife, and then some for skinning. A folding knife with two slender pointed blades, not unlike the type Blake and Lamb used to make, is a very good knife for skinning. A high-quality, very small sheath knife also has it uses. I no longer carry my skinning knives out on the trap line, as I have lost many a favorite knife while on the trap line, and lamented the loss. Keep them at home, safe and sound, so they will be there when you need them. You should also have a set of honing stones to keep your knives sharp. Dull knives are both dangerous and ineffective.

Binocular

A good binocular can be used to check your sets at a distance. Not only will it save time, but it also keeps human scent and presence at a minimum, especially with snow cover. Try to buy the best quality you can afford, with at least 8x power. Clarity and compactness is more important than magnification. I have used a pocket-sized Zeiss 8x binocular for years, and they have served me well both hunting and trapping.

Skinning Gambrel

This is a device that holds your catch properly while you are skinning. It is a narrow bar with two chains connected to a central point or ring. It is hung by the ring from above so the animal is at a convenient height for skinning. At the ends of the bar are hooks to which you attach the furbearer's back legs or hocks. This makes skinning so much easier and safer; it is well worth having one.

Tail Splitting Guides

This is a device that you place the furbearer's tail into. It has a slot that allows you to cut and split the tail exactly in a straight line.

Tail Stripper

When skinning a furbearer—the raccoon comes quickly to mind—you partially skin the tail downward from the base, and then you have to remove the tail bone from the rest of the tail. This handy little device makes the process easier and results in a better quality pelt, as opposed to just using your fingers.

Fleshing Tools

There are a few different types, used on different animals. They are available from most trapping supply houses, or you can make them yourself. They are used for removing unwanted fat and flesh left on the pelt after skinning, without damaging the pelt.

Fleshing Beam

This is a smooth long board, with rounded sides, and is round and pointed at one end. You will end up with a variety of boards, each a different width, for different size animals. The hide is slid over the board, fur side in, and allows you to flesh a section at a time by rotating the hide when you are done with fleshing each section, until complete. A well-made fleshing board makes fleshing an animal's pelt much easier and faster, not to mention the fact that it enables you to do a better job. Be sure to remove any burrs or stickers from the fur before fleshing.

Drying Frames or Stretchers

These are wire or wood frames that you use after the hide has been fleshed, in order to dry the hide so it will maintain its original shape and size. They come in different sizes for different species and sizes of animals. It is well advised to place the cased hide to the correct size frame, rather than try to force or stretch the hide to fit a larger frame. I much prefer the wire type over the wood. The wire type is lighter, easier to store, does not rot, and makes it easier to remove the animal's hide when the time comes.

Catchpole

A catchpole is a device that allows you to control a trapped animal that you may intend to release unharmed. It is usually made up of a four-foot-long piece of metal tubing with a cable running through the tubing, creating a loop or snare at one end, which you control, and which is placed around the animal's neck. They are easy to make, and every trapper should have one at his disposal.

Compass

This can be a life saver! A compass does one thing and one thing *only*; it points to magnetic North. This little bit of information, especially when exploring unfamiliar territory, can make the difference whether you spend a long time walking in circles (possibly spending the night in the woods) or making it back to your vehicle safely. Hundreds of times when I was coon hunting (done primarily in the dark), we would follow the hounds as they were on the trail of a raccoon, in so many directions we lost track which way was back to the truck. Without a compass, we had no way of knowing what direction to walk, and even more important, we wouldn't have had a means of staying on the correct heading, and not walking in circles. Some of the places we hunted, we had never even been there in daylight. What we would do before we left the road is take a reading and establish the general direction of the road. For example, if the road generally went in an east–west direction, and we were hunting on the north side of the road, we then knew that wherever we were, if you traveled south you would get back to the road. You may not come out onto the road exactly where you were parked; but nevertheless you were back on the road. A compass can weigh as little as an ounce, be the size of a quarter, and the price of a decent one can be as little as $10 to $15. I prefer the liquid-filled type. I strongly suggest you purchase one and practice with it *before* you set out in unfamiliar territory. Conditions can change even familiar places; heavy blinding snow fall, for example, can make a place that you thought you knew well look completely different. Another tip: When going into vast areas, if possible always tell someone your plans, so if you do not show up they have an idea where to start looking for you. In adverse conditions, this can make the difference between life and death.

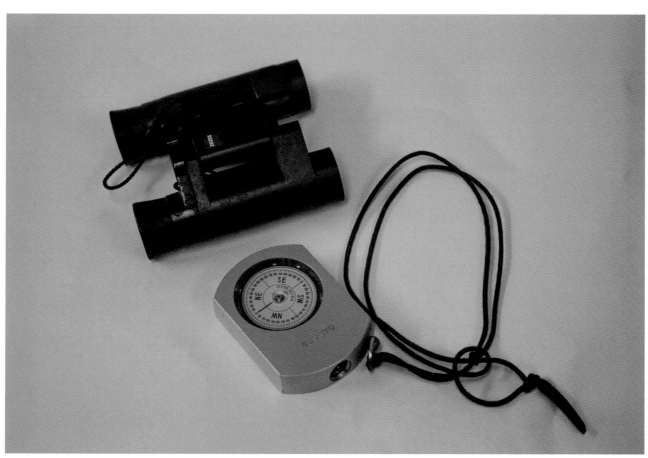

A small binocular—like these Zeiss 8x20s—and a compass are two tools that don't take up much room, but are well appreciated when needed.

GPS Units

Handheld GPS units, once you learn how to use them to their full potential, are a valuable addition to trap-line equipment. They can give you information that you can capitalize on to make your trap line so much more productive. Not only will they tell you where you are and how to get back to where you started, they will store exact positions of all your sets and how to get to them from where you are standing. They do have their limitations; you must have line of sight to the satellites that they work off of. They also work on batteries, so if the batteries fail, so does the GPS. They are by no means a replacement for a good compass!

Flagging

I always carry a small roll of surveyors flagging to mark a spot near my sets. This really comes in handy, especially I'm trapping near water sources with rising water levels, and after snow falls, when I'm trying to retrieve my traps.

A sturdy vessel and an outdoor fire are best for treating your traps.

Part 3

Trap Preparation—Give Yourself Every Advantage

Even the most expensive and highest quality traps are going to need some attention and tender loving care; it's this part of the trapper's labors that will make a huge difference in success. The best-laid plans and the most diligent trap set will be undermined by a trap that is not fully prepared; you want your traps to be treated and tuned to give the optimum performance, especially when trapping predators. The traps must be treated to remove the odor of metal and other foreign scents, as well as to prevent rusting when buried in the set. A waxed trap is a faster trap, and faster traps catch more animals by preventing losses. A properly waxed trap can and will be ready for service for a number of seasons, if properly stored.

Traps—and all associated parts, such as stakes, swivels, chain, grapples, slip links, and so on—should all be treated simultaneously. When I refer to traps in this section, I am referring to all these parts. Should you need to treat additional swivels, chains, or grapples, you may use the methods described below for any part of the equation.

This portion of trap preparation will require large quantities of boiling water, and some source of heat (fire, propane, etc.). I highly recommend that you perform these steps outside, in a well-ventilated area, away from any combustible materials. For example, trap wax is highly flammable, so do not try to use it on the kitchen stove (please don't ask how I learned this lesson). Safety first, please, with all the chemicals

and solutions you'll be using for treating your traps and equipment.

When treating traps during these processes, you want to open the trap jaws slightly, and place one of the chain links between the trap jaws before submerging your traps into any of the solutions. This will allow the entire surface of the trap jaws to be treated. A short length of wire can be bent into a hook, so you may fish the trap out of the solution. When you handle the traps from this point forward, use a pair of odorless rubber gloves; you absolutely do not want to touch them with bare skin.

Cleaning/Rusting

New traps are shipped with a coat of rust preventative, and this must be removed initially. I like to wash my new traps in a small bucket of gasoline to remove the rust preventative, and then I rinse them thoroughly in soapy water, finally giving them a rinse in clean water.

They may also be cleaned by boiling in a solution of water and several pounds of sifted hardwood ashes (ten pounds to twenty gallons of water), allowing the traps to stand in the solution overnight. They must be boiled for at least one hour. The hardwood ash creates a sort of "lye" solution, which thoroughly cleans your traps. Again, rinse the traps thoroughly with clean water when done.

A new trap can still carry the rust preventative used in shipping; it must be removed.

This old Herter's trap may look terribly rusted, but the surface can be easily cleaned and dyed.

Once rinsed, I set the traps in a patch of high grass, so the moisture from the grass is easily transferred to the clean metal, helping it to develop a light coat of rust on the traps. The objective is to develop an even, fine coating of rust on all surfaces of the trap, so the dye will adhere easily and evenly during the dyeing process.

Check your traps every other day, possibly adding water to them in very dry conditions, to assure the rusting process is even, without having deep rust that will cause pitting. If your traps aren't rusting fast enough, you may spray them with vinegar to speed up the process. The overall goal of this process is to "rough up" the metal.

De-Rusting

Once a trap is roughed up, whether by the above method or simply from age and prior seasons of use, the rust then needs to be removed before dyeing and waxing. Older traps that have wax on them from the previous seasons must be cleaned of all old treatment. The de-rusting process will remove this old material. There are several methods of de-rusting/cleaning a trap, and I'll highlight a couple here.

My favorite method, using the natural materials I have available in the Northeast, is using some tree bark from those species that contain a high amount of tannic acid. Hemlock and white oak bark are two of my favorites. As a point of note, the word "tanning," as in tanned leather, comes from the German word "*tanna*," which translates to oak. Additionally, the town of Tannserville, New York, got its name from the high volume leather tannery located there, due to an abundance of hemlock trees in the Catskill Mountains.

The bark of hemlock or white oak needs to be chopped finely and mixed with water at a ratio of five pounds of bark to twenty gallons of water. Boil the mixture for several hours (a minimum of three), and then strain the solution (with no bark) into a secondary bucket. Soak your traps in this solution for several days, and you'll see the rust removed. If you don't have access to these species of trees, you may research the native species in your area, to see which have a high tannic acid content, and substitute those for the hemlock/oak choice.

Another method is to bury the traps in muck, comprised of white oak and/or alder leaves and swampy soil, leaving the traps in this mixture for a month or until the rust is removed. This was a favorite method of many of the older trappers I grew up with in the 1960s; this method was used in the early twentieth century, and I've used it myself. It's a long process, so I suggest you begin in the early summer, allowing enough time for the process to work. Obviously, the bark method is faster, and in this busy world it's the method I prefer.

Tuning Your Traps

Many traps are made well, and could be used right out of the box, but I prefer to tune my traps for the best performance. This includes some filing of parts, trimming of pans, adjusting the mechanical parts of the trap, and so on.

Pans (for Coil-Spring Land Traps)

For some applications—particularly foxes and coyotes—it is advantageous to narrow the width of the trap pan to ensure the fox or coyote can only trigger the trap by stepping on the center of the trap; a smaller pan eliminates the possibility of a clean miss or just a pinched toe. By using a smaller pan, as shown on the trap below, I have increased my success rate dramatically.

The trap pan can be trimmed with a good, sharp pair of tin snips, followed by some filing of the edges to smooth the overall profile.

Some traps use a nut and bolt with a washer on the outside of the pan post. I prefer to install an additional brass washer on the inside of the pan post, which acts as a tension adjustment, as well as eliminating any pan wobble. A rigid pan, with no wobble, and the brass washer installed makes adjusting the pan tension much easier; it will hold adjustment much better. I prefer to have the pan shank riding against a washer, rather than just the pan post. Now

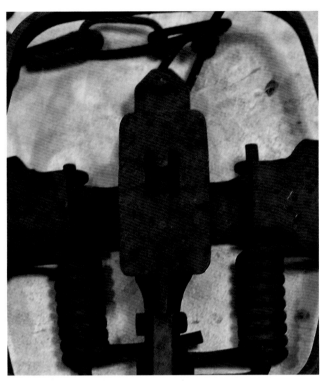

is a good time to set the pan tension, whether heavier tension for water sets, or a lighter tension for dirt hole sets.

The bolt-nut which attaches the pan shank to the pan post can be adjusted to achieve the desired tension. You can use a small section of steel pipe or common tools as a weight; simply weigh the object, and adjust the bolt until the object of desired weight trips the trigger. Gingerly set the weighted object on the center of the pan, and adjust the nut until it sets the trap off. The process works much better with a partner. Your makeshift weight needs to be tall enough to prevent your fingers from being caught in your own trap during the adjustment process.

Your trap pans should be adjusted to be perfectly level, when the trap is on a level surface. Having a tilted pan may result in a poorly functioning trap. Use a couple pairs of pliers—one to hold the pan

The pan of this Herter's trap has been cut down, for better performance.

Testing the pan tension on a coil spring trap.

and one to bend it into adjustment—to set the pan level.

Dogs and pan shank notches

The first point of attention I give is to the dog loop or eye; I want my dogs to rotate freely, yet have very little lateral play. This can be done with a large pair of pliers, used to tighten the dog loop or eye down; should you over-tighten, a flat-head screwdriver will easily reopen the eye to readjust.

Trap dogs are usually stamped steel, and depending on the manufacturing process, the end of the dog can be less than perfect.

Dog ends should be perfectly square, and free of burrs. A good file can be used to create a perfectly square and straight dog, removing any burrs, or high spots, and ensuring that the dog end—crucial to having a well-tuned trap—is absolutely square and crisp.

The same concept is applicable to the pan shank notch, which makes contact with the dog end. The pan shank notch should be filed to a burr-free state, with sharp right-angle corners.

This stage is a good time to lengthen or shorten your trap chains, add additional swivels and/or slip links, and attach your identification tags, if required by local law.

A trap's dog, as it comes from the factory, out of square.

The pan shank notch, as delivered from the factory.

A little bit of filing can greatly improve performance, as shown here on a properly tuned trap.

Dyeing the traps

Dyeing a trap is the first part of the process which prevents rust and helps to cover the scent of steel. The dyeing process can be completed with a couple of possible methods. My personal favorite—more than likely due to a tight family budget as a younger man—is to use a blend (one or more of the following) of natural materials. The ripe, red berries of a sumac—as you'll find them in late summer and early autumn—combined with the ripened hulls of black walnuts, some finely chopped maple, hemlock or walnut bark, and chopped hemlock boughs have dyed my traps for decades.

I use a ratio of one pound of material to two gallons of water. Once the water is boiling, add the material, allowing the mixture to boil for at least thirty minutes, and then submerge the traps, adding a bit more material over the traps. Allow the traps to simmer in the solution for at least two hours, allowing them to stand overnight in the cooling solution.

The following morning, bring the solution back to a simmer—not a rolling boil—as this will remove any of the natural material that may have adhered to the traps as they cooled the previous evening. As the traps stand—even without the wax—they

Hemlock boughs, sumac berries, and maple bark can make a great trap dye.

Philip J. Massaro adding hard wood ashes to the boiling mixture.

Adding the rusted traps to the boiling dye mixture.

will not rust for several months, though the wax is a necessary portion. Remember, use your odorless rubber gloves if you must handle the treated traps; it is imperative that you don't get your scent on a treated trap. A wire hook is a much better means of handling traps.

As an alternative method, many commercial trapping supply stores offer logwood dye crystals to dye traps; the method works well and is fast. Just be sure to carefully follow the directions from the manufacturer, as each type is different.

Whichever method you choose, the best time to wax the traps is just after the dyeing process is completed, and the trap is thoroughly dried. This is another reason why I prefer to bring my dye solution to a simmer again the following morning, as it heats the metal and allows it to dry evenly and quickly. I either hang my traps on a line or tree branch to dry, or you may optionally set them on a clean board.

Waxing the Traps

Waxing your traps keeps your equipment rust-free nearly indefinitely, and will speed up the lock time of the trap jaws, as all the moving parts are now lubricated. There are a few types of wax and methods of application that trappers have traditionally used—and it's been a source of argument among veteran trappers. Let's look at these ideas, and examine the pros and cons.

Firstly, the type of wax you use makes a difference. Pure paraffin wax is the least advantageous; it is not as durable as beeswax or a paraffin/beeswax combination will be. Commercially produced "odorless trap wax"—the content of which may vary, depending on the manufacturer—is suitable, though in my experience I have had the best results with pure *bleached* beeswax. I emphasize the bleached beeswax, versus ordinary beeswax, as the latter contains the scent of honey, which the predators will smell, and

Odorless trap wax.

inevitably dig out your trap. You may read advice which states that the type of wax is irrelevant, but I am a firm proponent of pure, bleached beeswax, which can be obtained from many different suppliers. It's more expensive, but well worth the price paid.

Secondly, the method of waxing is as important as the type of wax chosen. When I was a teenager, a well-intended trapper instructed me as to the process of waxing my traps. He was simply wrong, and I do not recommend this process, though I feel it deserves explanation so you can avoid it. His process was as follows: In a container measuring ten inches in diameter and at least twelve inches in depth, add eight inches of water and two pounds of paraffin wax. Heat the mixture nearly to a boil, until the wax is thoroughly melted. Take each trap individually, and submerge it in the heated solution until the trap attains the temperature of the solution. Draw the trap slowly upward—as the wax will stay on top of the water—so the wax will adhere to the metal as it is pulled up through the wax. This method has two major drawbacks: one, the paraffin wax is too soft for prolonged use, and two, the water at the bottom of the container prevents the wax from adhering evenly across the trap's surfaces. I ended up with water spots and bubbles on the surface of my traps, with the wax eventually peeling off as a result of this method of application. My personal method has given much better results.

What I use is 100 percent bleached beeswax—though most trappers use a blend of one part bleached beeswax to two parts paraffin—or the commercial odorless trap wax, in either black or white; all are acceptable with my application method, though my preference is definitely 100 percent bleached beeswax. I wax my traps individually in a stainless-steel pot which is deeper than it is wide—as a narrow pot requires less wax—and melt enough wax in the pot until I have approximately ten inches of liquid wax heated. For each five pounds of wax I've melted in my pot, I add a pea-sized ball (the size of a common pencil eraser) of pine pitch; this helps the wax

adhere to the trap, in addition to hardening the wax slightly. Remember, use only a pea-sized ball of pitch, nothing bigger; too much pitch and it will make the wax gummy and unusable. The pitch isn't a necessity, but I've used it for years and have come to rely on it.

I bring the bleached beeswax to a boil, and using my long wire hook, I submerge the trap in wax for five minutes—allowing the metal to come to the temperature of the melted wax—and then rotate the trap in the wax to ensure complete coverage. I then slowly draw the trap out of the wax and hang it to dry in an odorless area, so the wax can cool and harden. If the trap is destined for land trapping—especially for trapping predators—I place each trap in a gallon re-sealable freezer bag once the trap is completely cooled. This keeps any foreign odors off my traps; they will be clean and ready for use. As a further precaution for fox and coyote trapping, I will dip the head of my trap stakes in the melted wax.

Note: I prefer to heat wax on a propane flame, as it allows me to control the temperature much better than by building a fire. Wax is extremely flammable, and I don't want to overheat my wax. Additionally, the use of a propane heat source eliminates the risk of having your traps obtain the odor of wood smoke during the final waxing process. Remember, the goal is to have your traps as odorless as possible.

At this stage, your traps are ready for the field.

Storage of Traps

Let's start with a list of "nevers," regarding trap storage. Never store traps in a garage, never store traps in your house, never store traps in the trunk of a car, never store traps in a barn inhabited by animals, never store traps in a shed that has gasoline, oil, mowers, snow blowers, and so on. The idea, once again, is to keep them from being exposed to foreign odors.

I use an odor-free outbuilding for storage, and built a wooden chest for storage, the bottom of which I lined with pine and hemlock boughs. This is extremely important for land traps; the water traps will be submerged, and are not as sensitive to the foreign odors, as they will be submerged once set.

Transportation of Traps and Equipment

When transporting your equipment, the clean, open bed of a pickup truck (free from any petroleum products) is best; but not everyone owns a truck. If you own a car or SUV, I recommend you build a wooden chest—lined with evergreen boughs—that will fit the vehicle's storage area. A plastic storage tote, with a sealed cover, makes a sensible alternative.

Keep your scents and lures in a separate container—a plastic bucket with cover makes a good choice—to prevent any transmission of odor onto the traps you've worked so hard to prepare.

Part 4

The Animals

Foxes

"Crazy like a fox." You've heard the phrase before, and it rings completely true. Their actions can be confusing, mystifying, and sometimes downright genius. That brilliant mind is what makes a fox so difficult to trap, and if you want to measure your skills as a trapper, focus on foxes and you'll see your weak points rather quickly. A good fox trapper is a good trapper, hands down.

Vulpes vulpes, or *Vulpes fulva*—the red fox—populates much of North America and Europe, and its fur has been prized for centuries. His smaller cousin, the gray fox—*Urocyon cinereoargenteus*—is confined to North America. Sometimes referred to as a "wood gray," because it will frequently climb the lower sections of trees, the gray fox has a beautiful coat, though it is generally less desirable than a prime "cherry red."

Red Foxes

The red fox weighs between ten and thirty pounds, depending on area and food, and will measure two to three feet from nose to tail, with a tail measuring ten

The red fox. (Photo Credit: Getty Images.)

to fifteen inches. They are extremely agile, capable of clearing a six-foot fence, and can slip through the smallest of holes in a fence to raid a chicken house; they are opportunists who will take full advantage of a free meal whenever possible. Red foxes vary in color from a yellowish-red to a deep cherry red, with signature black feet, and a contrasting white chest, belly, and tail tip. Fox fur is very soft, and equally warm, with long hair that insulates the animal during even the harshest of winters. The red fox has five digits on its forepaws, and four on its rear paws, with non-retractable claws like a dog. Red foxes breed once annually during late winter/early spring, with two to twelve pups (sometimes referred to as "kits") being born seven to eight weeks later. Nine days after birth in the den—often an improved woodchuck or badger hole—their eyes will open and they will remain in the den for about four to ten weeks, depending on the size of the litter. The young will stay with the parents until early winter, when they head out on their own, with the male leaving briefly as the vixen nears the time of birth. Breeding pairs of foxes will often use the same den for years. Foxes in the wild have a lifespan of about four years, with some specimens in captivity living as long as seven years.

Foxes have an average home range of approximately three to four miles, and expelled pups can disperse as far as fifty miles from their birth place, with most staying within ten miles of the birth den. A red fox's diet consists primarily of field mice, with squirrels, rabbits, voles, birds (including game birds), insects (they love grasshoppers), young woodchucks, and the occasional fruits and berries. They are the scourge of poultry farmers, often wreaking havoc on domesticated birds like chickens and ducks. A smart trapper will look to the areas in which the fox's prey animals thrive; the farmed fields—and their adjoining hedge rows—are the haunts of woodchucks, rabbits, mice, and game birds, and therefore foxes as well.

While it is an efficient predator, the fox is not exactly at the top of the food chain. Coyotes, lynx, and eagles will all kill foxes—with the coyote being especially fond of cleaning an area out of red foxes—and man, with his sprawling development, has taken his toll on red foxes as well. The red fox prefers using the cover of night to do the majority of its hunting, but may be found in broad daylight, going about its business.

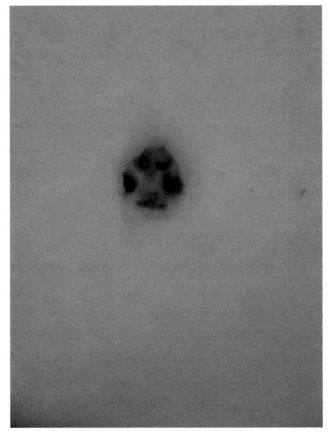

Red fox track in snow.

Red fox scat on fresh dirt.

The gray fox, climber of trees. (Photo Credit: Getty Images.)

Gray Foxes

The gray fox is smaller than the red fox (about three pounds lighter), weighing seven to eleven pounds, and measuring an average overall length of just about three feet.

It populates the southern areas of the North American continent, from coast to coast, with the northern limits being from New England and New Brunswick, to the southern parts of Wyoming and again northerly into Oregon. They are found as far south as southern Mexico, down into the Yucatan peninsula. The gray fox uses a different style of den than his red cousin, preferring hollowed trees and logs, as well as some rocky hillsides that provide nooks and crannies for a den. Gray foxes have a litter of two to five kits on average, with birth taking place from mid-March to June, depending upon the latitude. Their mating habits are very similar to the red fox, and pups will appear outside the den at six to seven weeks of age. Young gray foxes leave their parents in the early autumn, with the parents often remaining together for the next mating season. The young don't travel as far away from their birth place as the red foxes will, usually staying within a few miles of their parent's

den. Once the female has chosen her mate, she will likely keep him for life, using the same den throughout the year as a base of operations, unlike the red fox. The lifespan of the gray fox is the same as that of the red fox. A gray fox has the same paw configuration as the red (five frontal digits and four rear digits), yet the coloration is entirely different. Its very name—*Urocyon cinereoargenteus*—translates to "ashen-silver," denoting the color of the gray fox's coat. The tail also differs from that of a red fox in that it is comprised entirely of guard hairs, with a lack of soft underfur. A gray fox can have a "collar" of orangey fur, with the same color on the inside of the ear base at the skull.

The gray fox earned its nickname "wood gray" for its willingness and ability to climb trees as a means of escaping danger. It prefers the forests for its den sites, yet will be found feeding on much the same as the red fox. Among livestock, the gray fox can and will be a selfish and wasteful killer. Many stories abound regarding the killing of newborn lambs, where the fox cleverly kills and opens a small hole in the paunch of the lamb, eating only the liver, and leaving the rest to the other scavengers.

Gray foxes suffer from the same predation by larger animals that red foxes do, and quite a few

The gray fox, with collar of lighter colored fur. (Photo Credit: Getty Images.)

times I've found only the front leg and shoulder left in my trap; a coyote had come during the night and robbed me of my prize, leaving only scraps after his meal. The red fox and the gray fox are mortal enemies; where their territories overlap, problems can and will occur.

How To Find Them

Looking for fox sign is paramount to being a successful trapper. Preseason scouting is as important as any step in the equation; if you're trying to trap an animal that isn't present, the best sets in the world will result in failure. Foxes love the edges of different terrains; it could be the edges of a hay lot or corn field, a belt of old timber where it meets a young woods, hedgerows between crop fields or open meadows—all are the haunts of the fox.

Woods, roads, stream beds, sandy areas, small clearings in the woods, and frozen streams and lakes are great places to look for fox sign. Often I have tracked a fox meandering from bank to bank on a small frozen stream while hunting through the woods; I've also seen their tracks along muddy wood roads, using it much as a human would. A fox will leave its scat on small grass mounds, ant hills, old hay bales, or exposed rocks, much as a dog will. Their tracks are easy to identify, as it will appear that the feet are moving in a straight line in the snow, rather than being offset the width of the body like a dog's tracks. If there are ponds in the area you intend to trap, look to the dyke surrounding the pond for fox spoor and scat; they simply love to use these areas for "fox toilets." They love the short, cropped fields where their keen sense of hearing and smell can be used to find mice running under the snow, or in the short grass.

I always carry a small bucket or shoulder pouch during my preseason scouting, with plenty of various sized plastic freezer bags, and use those to collect

This farmland, with its open fields full of mice and woods for cover, makes a perfect habitat for foxes.

mouse nests, old bird's nests, fox scat, etc., for use in my sets during trapping season. A roll of surveyor's flagging can be used to mark sites for future sets. A handheld GPS unit can also be used to mark and record areas that have good fox sign, or to mark those ant hills that hold the soil that comes in so handily when temperatures plummet.

Equipment for Fox Trapping

Traps

I have had the best success—with the least amount of problems—when using a No. 1¾ or No. 2 double coil spring trap for foxes. Avoid using double long spring traps, as these types of traps are larger and heavier to carry, and take up an excessive amount of room in the trap bed. Jump traps aren't ideal either,

as the trap will invariably move as it goes off, and I've learned the hard way that using a jump trap can result in a miss, or a toe-hold on the fox. The jump trap is better suited for raccoons or water furbearers. I've long been a fan of the No. 1¾ double coil spring, as it is a bit faster than the No. 2; the jaws are smaller, and will come together quicker as there is less distance to cover. Foxes are quick and the trap must be quicker.

I tune my fox traps in the following manner, as it has made a definite difference in trap performance. I file the end of the dog to remove the curl left from the manufacturing process. I want the top of the dog to be either a perfect right angle or slightly acute, when viewed from the side. This results in a crisp trigger, removing any creep when a fox steps on the pan. I also adjust the pan tension to about eight ounces,

The No. 2 Herter's and No. 1¾ Oneida Victor coil spring traps are both excellent for fox.

as this will take a fox even with a light step. The pan tension can be measured with an inexpensive trigger weight gauge used for rifles.

Some trappers cut down the surface area of the pan, to eliminate the possibility of the fox setting the trap off while stepping on both the pan and the jaw simultaneously. I've done this, and feel it's a good idea, as it ensures that the fox's foot is centered in the trap when he sets it off; guaranteeing a firm hold on the paw.

All fox traps should use at least three swivels, one at either end of the trap chain, and one more in the middle of the chain. Attach a lap link or quick link to the end of the trap chain, to attach the stake. A clean, dyed, and waxed trap is paramount when it comes to fox trapping, and be absolutely certain never to touch your fox traps with bare hands. Do not allow them to be exposed to tobacco smoke or any other foreign odor.

Trap Stakes

Old-time fox trappers used wooden trap stakes, but I wouldn't recommend the practice at all. Steel stakes—preferably one-half-inch reinforcing bars, twenty to twenty-four inches in length—work best in normal autumn soil conditions. The stake should be sharpened to a point on one end and have a nut or washer welded to the other (I prefer it one-quarter to one-half-inch below the top, so the nut/washer and weld aren't hit by the hammer when setting the stake), to attach the trap chain. Just below the nut or washer, I grind off an inch or two of the distressed portion of the rebar to allow the lap link or quick link at the end of the chain to swivel freely, with no resistance. Your stakes should be dyed and waxed in the same manner as your traps.

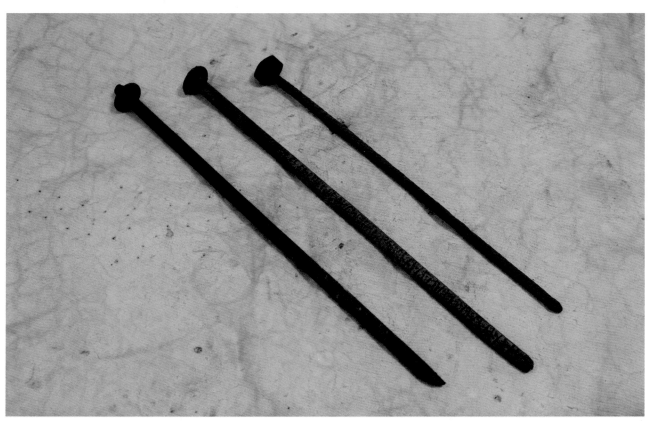

These sturdy stakes, made of reinforcing rod, are a good design for fox.

Trap stake with smoothed area just below the washer.

Tools

Trowel, both narrow and wide

Sifter

Gloves

Hoe

Hatchet or ax (for cutting, notching, and
hammering)

Pliers and screwdriver

Drop cloth

Urine spray bottle

Cotton balls

Trap pan covers

Trap basket or bucket

Grapples

Spare quick links, lap links, and chain (with
swivels installed)

Lure bottles

Pick hammer

Bait fork

Fox Bait/Food Lure (Mouse-Based)

This is my favorite bait for foxes. Though there are many good commercially made baits, I prefer making my own.

This fox bait/food lure works very well on foxes. If you are an inexperienced trapper and this is your first or second year of trapping, I strongly advise that you buy your lure and baits. You can refer back to this recipe when you have become proficient with the various sets. You need everything in your favor when just starting out with foxes, and worrying about bait/lure making should be last on your list. Concentrate on proper trap sets, and scouting, and leave the lure bait making to the professionals for the time being. There are many sound lures and baits available today that were not available when I started trapping. I was a young teenager, about the age of thirteen, and everybody I knew who trapped was much older than me. They guarded their recipes for baits and lures like

Trapped mice can be frozen for fox bait.

they were military secrets. I guess they figured I would not execute the sets properly and if I used their recipe I would just educate all the foxes in the area. When I finally obtained a bottle of gland lure and a quart of fox urine, I guarded it as if it were gold. It was gold to me! There is another recipe that works equally as well on foxes in the chapter on coyote trapping.

Ingredients

1 dozen fresh, frozen mice. I trap them all winter, spring, and summer, and freeze them whole for future use as I need them.

½ lb. of fresh, finely chopped muskrat meat and glands, no bones or guts.

If you cannot get the fresh muskrat carcass, you can obtain one from a road kill and freeze it until ready for use. If you cannot obtain a muskrat carcass at all, use the meat and glands form a road-killed woodchuck, but muskrat is preferred.

1 tbsp. of powdered, roasted deer hooves.*

*If you cannot obtain deer hooves, you can substitute with the hoof trimmings from a horse, goat, sheep, or cow. All of these work just as well. What you do is take the hoof trimmings or whole hooves, just the nail parts, and wrap them up in aluminum foil and roast them on a grill or fire until they are totally roasted, charred, and crumble easily, and ground them into a powder.

3 tbsp. sodium benzoate
3 oz. fox urine
3 oz. glycerin

Take your one-half pound of muskrat meat and chop very fine. Place the meat in a jar, place a cloth or cheese cloth over the top, and lightly screw the lid on so that no flies can get in and the gases can escape the jar. Plastic is safer than glass, as it will not break from expanding gases. Just make sure the jar is odorless and clean. Place in a dark spot, at room temperature, and let it taint for six days.

Two days after you started to prepare your muskrat meat, take your frozen mice and chop them up as fine as you can.

It is easier to chop them up frozen rather than thawed, as it makes less of a mess. You can use an old hand crank meat grinder rather than chopping up the mice and meat. It really makes a mess in the grinder and I would rather just chop them up finely, though either way works well.

Place the frozen pieces of mice in a jar, cover in the same manner as the muskrat meat, and let stand at room temperature and taint for four days.

Now mix the two thoroughly. It is much easier to mix the two in a bowl, rather than trying to mix them in the jar. Now add a heaping tablespoon of the roasted hooves, and again mix well. Next add your fox urine and again mix well. Next blend in three tablespoons of sodium benzoate until completely mixed, and now add your three ounces of glycerin. Again, mix the entire batch until completely blended. Cover it with a lid, tightly. Store in a cool spot until you need it. Check next day to see if any gases have built up; if they have, it needs to be mixed more, with more sodium benzonate added. You can make an extra batch as instructed above, but add about eight drops of tincture of skunk, for use in colder temperatures.

One of the ways I utilize this bait/lure is: I put a small plug of dry grass in the bottom of a nine-inch-deep hole, then put a small amount of the above concoction (a teaspoon or so) on top of the grass plug. Cover this with another small grass plug. Next I take a whole frozen or freshly thawed mouse; I smear a generous amount of the above recipe all over the mouse or just dip the mouse in the jar and place it down the hole and cover the mouse with another loosely packed dry grass plug.

Trap Sets

The Dirt Hole Set
The dirt hole set is an emulation of a fox's various activities, including looking for food—mouse nests, ground squirrels, chipmunks, etc.—storing food for future use, or general investigation. It is the most

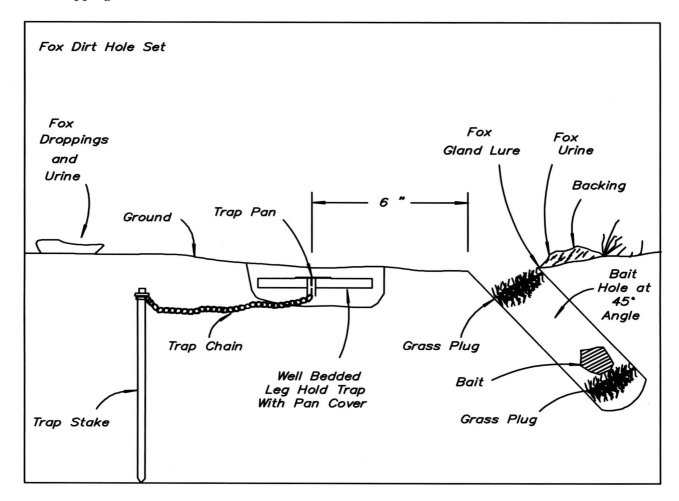

Fox Dirt Hole Set

Fox Droppings and Urine

Ground

Trap Pan

6 "

Fox Gland Lure

Fox Urine

Backing

Bait Hole at 45° Angle

Trap Chain

Well Bedded Leg Hold Trap With Pan Cover

Grass Plug

Bait

Grass Plug

Trap Stake

popular, and often the most misused and misunder-stood fox set. It is also one of the most effective meth-ods of fox trapping, because it takes full advantage of the fox's inquisitive nature. A fox is an opportunist, and will shamelessly rob the cache of another fox or animal. Therefore, we can beat him at his own game by using the dirt hole set to mimic a food cache, or simply create a situation where "curiosity killed the cat."

However, if done improperly or sloppily, you will simply educate the fox, making him all the more dif-ficult to trap, as he will quickly become suspicious of all dirt hole sets. Many effective baits and lures, of high quality, have been rendered useless by improper application in a dirt hole set. Take the utmost precau-tion when using the dirt hole set and it will quickly become a favorite, producing fur season after sea-son. The dirt hole set is a fluid set, in that the same exact approach need not be taken every time; this is a good opportunity to mix things up, so long as

you understand that it must be absolutely free of any human odor.

The general location of a dirt hole set will make or break the operation. Obviously, those areas with good fox sign, as discussed in the preseason scouting, will be the most productive, but once sign is located, the choice of specific placement is key. Foxes love the edges of large fields, cultivated or not, and especially love the points of hedge rows and woods. If there are ponds in the area, the dikes between them are great choice for a dirt hole set, as are the edges of hay lots where farmers have abandoned old hay bales, as they hold a prolific amount of mice. A large clearing in the woods can also be a good choice for a dirt hole, providing the soil is well-drained. Part of the secret is to choose a location where the fox feels comfortable and safe from humans or predators.

Getting more specific, you'll want to look for an open spot at least 20 feet in diameter, free of logs, underbrush, bushes, and taller grass, with an area that will drain away from your set. If need be, remove any of the above objects; some trappers prefer to mow the area with a small machete or scythe before season to make the area as natural as possible for the fox.

With your exact set location determined, you can now proceed, following these step-by-step set instructions.

We selected a level spot, at the highest point of this open meadow. Foxes will use the barway as a highway.

The trap shows where the set will be made.

This site has some thick sod that will need to be removed.

The trowel is used to dig the bait hole.

The pan location is measured out from the bait hole.

A trap stake is driven into one corner of the trap bed.

Dirt hole set with the trap in place.

The pan cover installed. Note the slit in the waxed paper for the dog.

The dirt that was removed from the trap bed is now gently sifted over the trap.

Fox (or coyote, depending on the set) urine is misted over the set.

Dry grass is then sifted over the set, to blend the site to the natural surroundings.

Wearing your rubber gloves to handle all tools (you never want to transfer scent), set your trap before you even approach the site. Always work downwind (breeze in your face) from your site if possible, and place your drop cloth so you can kneel without leaving any scent. If you're using rubber hip boots, be sure they cover your knees if you are not using the drop cloth to kneel on. Your drop cloth—whether it's being knelt upon or simply used to keep your tools, bucket, or basket from contacting the ground—should always have the same side on the ground, to keep the site as scent-free as possible. I prefer to carry a small plastic bucket to the site instead of the entire trap basket, as it is easier to keep this scent free, and can be washed between sets if necessary. I can carry one small setup in the bucket, and the remainder of my traps and tools will stay in my basket, fifty-plus feet away. I keep this bucket within arm's-length, on the drop cloth, for easy access. Once in position, stay there until the set is complete.

Using a hoe, clear out and scrape an egg-shaped to teardrop-shaped oval site, measuring fourteen inches wide by eighteen inches long, removing all sod and clumps of vegetation. This will house both the trap and the bait hole. Place the removed sod and vegetation on the drop cloth for future use and/or removal. At the pointed end of the site, dig an oval-shaped hole—three inches wide by five inches high, seven to nine inches deep—as close to a 45-degree angle to the ground as possible. This will serve as the bait hole. The dirt removed from the bait hole should be placed in the sifter for future use.

Next you need to scrape out the trap bed, the center of which should be approximately seven-inches from the bait hole and roughly two-inches deeper than the level of the site. The trap bed needs to be slightly larger than the footprint of your chosen trap. Tamp the trap bed with a stone or small hammer until the ground is firm. At this time, drive the trap stake—with trap attached—into one corner of the trap bed until the stake head is one-inch below the trap bed. Replace three-quarter inches of loose, stone-free dirt into the trap bed. Carefully place the trap into the loose dirt of the trap bed, with the center of the trap pan seven inches out from the edge of the bait hole and one to one and one-half inches offset from center. Using your gloved hands, firm up the dirt tightly around the outside of the trap, preventing the trap from shifting or moving within the trap bed. At this point, cover the pan with the pan cloth or cover, making sure that the tear in the cloth is properly aligned with the trigger.

Note: If using waxed paper for a pan cover, after cutting it to size, I usually crumple it up in my hand, and then reopen it up to the original size and shape, just before placing it on the pan trap. This will prevent it from producing any crinkling noise and alerting the fox if he steps near the trap. Foxes can and will hear this noise, and might dig up the trap without getting caught, or just walk away educated.

Using the dirt previously placed in the sifter, sift this soil over the entire trap bed to blend in the bed with the site, leaving no rises or depressions. With a small branch—I prefer a pine bough—brush the entire trap bed to make it look natural.

Next we must bait and lure the set. For this step, you must remove your gloves and place them back in the bucket or basket (I use a gallon-size sealable freezer bag to store my gloves), as you do not want bait or lure scent, or any other foreign odors, on your gloves. Using the bait fork or sharpened stick, place a walnut- to egg-sized piece of bait at the back of the bait hole. Cover the bait with a small amount of dirt, or as I prefer, a plug of dead grass, if available. Place six to ten drops of gland lure at the top edge of the bait hole, allowing some to fall onto the grass plug or cover dirt. One piece of bait is adequate, as our goal is to entice the fox to investigate the set, not to fatten it up.

Using your spray bottle filled with fox urine, spray a mist over the entire set, concentrating a few squirts into the bait hole. Though optional, I have found that using some dead grass, and the sifter as a grater, covering the entire set with finely grated grass

will not only break up the pattern, but will entice those foxes who've been previously educated to the dirt hole set to investigate further.

A call lure can be used to entice foxes from long distances. Place an absorbent article—a corn cob, a mouse's nest, a piece of boiled cloth, a large cotton ball, etc.—approximately twenty feet away from and upwind of the prevailing wind direction at a height of four feet above the ground. Apply ten drops of a good call lure (purchased from a trapping supply company) to the article, to allow the scent to disperse and bring the fox in to investigate the dirt hole set.

At this point, I'd like to share some subtleties that can make a significant difference in success. Regarding trap placement, I've learned—the hard way—that if using a trap placement that requires the fox to step over the jaw, as opposed to in-between the jaws, I place the triggered jaw toward the bait hole. This avoids the fox stepping on the trigger and pan simultaneously, which can push his paw upward and out of the trap as the trigger flies up to release the jaw. It's happened to me numerous times before someone educated me, and I hope it prevents you from having to learn the hard way. Another common mistake is placing the trap too close to the bait hole. It's better to have the trap farther away than to be too close.

I've also learned to dress up and vary my dirt hole sets by placing fox scat—previously collected while scouting—on the outside edge of the of the dirt hole pattern, and giving it a quick squirt of fox urine, as a visual and olfactory attractor and as a suspicion remover.

I've adorned my bait hole plug with small bird feathers, in an attempt to recreate a situation where a fox has taken a bird. I've also used rabbit and deer fur, or other small pieces of natural fur, such as a squirrel tail, to add variety to my dirt hole sets. If four days go by without activity, I re-spray the site with fox urine, to keep it fresh; I'll also reapply my gland lure every eight or nine days, possibly more frequently if it's been raining.

Hopefully, you'll be skinning a fox before long, and you'll need to re-build your set after a catch.

Once you've dispatched the fox you've trapped, you'll see a torn-up circle where the animal worked to escape, but was restrained by the trap, chain, and stake. Remove the fox from the torn-up area immediately and with great intensity inspect the torn-up area and remove any and all—no matter how small— drops or clots of blood. The presence of decomposed blood in your set will prompt another visiting animal to dig and roll in the bloodied area, which can spoil the entire setup by springing the trap, leaving you with nothing more than a flipped-up trap. Use the trowel to dig underneath any blood-soaked soil, and cast that soil away from your site. Remove any dirt within the site that has been contaminated with bait, lure, or blood. This will include cleaning the surface of the bait hole, and covering the bait again; the bait may be reused in the hole, you may want to freshen it. Re-level the soil at the site with your hoe, and if you plan to reuse the same trap, remove all blood and hair from the entire trap with a fox urine–soaked rag. I personally change to a clean trap, and put the used trap in a gallon freezer bag, so I can clean and re-wax it at home. Utilizing the original bait hole if possible, prepare the site as described above. Place bait back in the hole, but you'll need a few drops of gland lure, as the previous catch will have dispersed its natural scents. Any droppings that resulted from the catch

Gray fox in a dirt set, from the late 1970s.

can be placed on the edge of the pattern, as a natural attractant.

If you trap a species other than fox in this set, I would recommend you abandon the site, starting over a few yards away. The former site will be a general attractor, but the new dirt hole will not smell of other animals.

The Mound or Ant Hill Set

This set is one of the easiest sets to construct, catches those foxes that are shy of the dirt hole sets, and is nearly dog-proof. It uses the fox's natural wariness

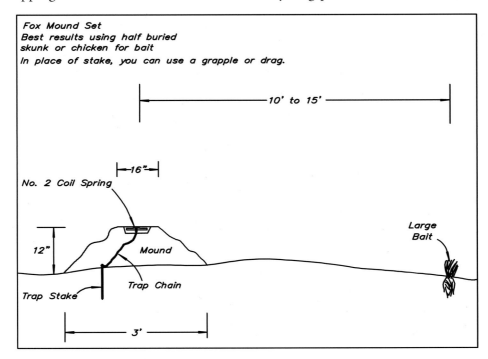

Fox Mound Set
Best results using half buried
skunk or chicken for bait
In place of stake, you can use a grapple or drag.

10' to 15'

16"

No. 2 Coil Spring

Large
Bait

12"

Mound

Trap Chain

Trap Stake

3'

and curiosity to investigate an attractant, to the trapper's advantage. Foxes simply love to use small mounds or humps to gain an elevation advantage when investigating that which they find interesting. I prefer to use a natural attractant such as a half-buried skunk or rabbit, a deer tail, a muskrat carcass, or a squirrel tail, all except the skunk with some call lure on it. The principal is to have the fox circle the attractant, and ultimately use the mound for a visual advantage, where it will be caught in your trap.

Ant hills make a wonderful choice, as their natural condition offers excellent drainage, and the soil simply will not freeze. Ant hill soil is prized by fox trappers, and is often harvested and kept for use in other sets, especially in truly cold conditions. Find an ant hill no higher than eighteen inches tall, and eighteen to twenty-four inches in diameter or larger at the top, for this set. If no ant hills are present,

you can construct your own mound, or take advantage of other natural formations like rotted stumps. Open areas, like cattle pasture, hay lots, or even harvested grain fields are a good place to look for these mounds or ant hills to be effective. A large clearing in the woods, where old stumps have rotted, is also a good location for this set. What you're looking for is an area with a 360-degree view, for at least twenty feet, preferably more.

Stake Method, on an Ant Hill

Dig out an area two inches bigger than the footprint of your trap—I prefer a No. 1¾ or No. 2 double coil spring for this set—on the top of the mound, about five inches deep, and save that precious material for future use.

You'll need a trap stake two feet in length or longer, and drive it down in the center of the hill, as far

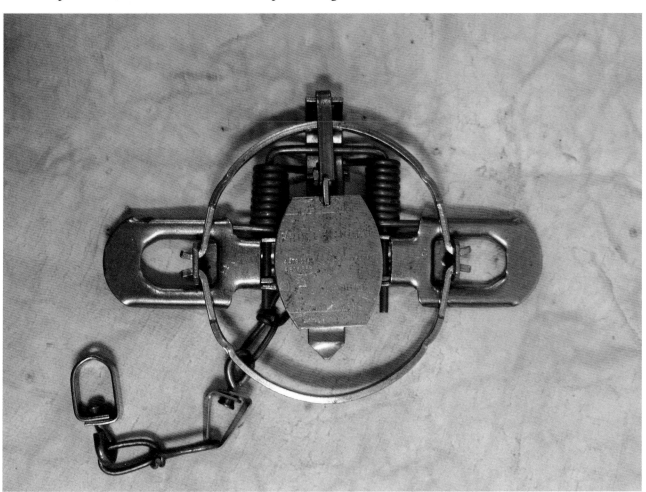

The 1¾ coil spring, perfect for the ant hill set.

as possible. Attach your trap with a trap chain that's three feet in length, possibly a bit longer, as you want the fox, once caught, to be pulling perpendicular to the axis of the trap stake rather than straight up. Coil the trap chain on top of the stake, at the bottom of the five-inch-deep area, and backfill with soil until within an inch of the top of the mound. Level the base of the dug-out area, and tamp the soil firm. Carefully place the pre-set trap on the tamped area of the trap bed. Using your gloved hands, firm up the previously collected ant hill dirt tightly around the outside of the trap, preventing the trap from shifting or moving within the trap bed. At this point, cover the pan with the pan cloth or cover, making sure that the tear in the cloth is properly aligned with the trigger.

Using your sifter, cover the trap with sifted dirt which you removed from the mound, to make it equal to or slightly higher than the original height of the mound. Smooth this loose material with a pine bough or small broom to blend it in. On the edge of the ant hill, place a couple a dozen drops of fox urine. Place your attractor ten to thirty feet away. Again, it's a simple concept, but very effective, especially in frigid temperatures when others fail.

Drag Method, on an Ant Hill

This is very similar to the above method, except your trap hole is only two inches deep instead of five, as we'll be wiring the trap chain to a drag instead of using a stake. Take a length of clean No. 9 wire or heavier, and push it down the center of your trap bed at a 45-degree angle until it exits the side of the base of the ant hill. Attach one end of the wire to your trap chain and the other end of this wire firmly to the center of a four- to five-foot-long, four-inch-diameter log, to serve as a drag. Pull on the drag end of the wire until the end of the trap chain is firm against the trap bed at the top of the ant hill. Bed and cover trap in the same manner previously described above, using urine and attractor in the same manner.

The Constructed Mound

This method works best in a cultivated field, such as a harvested cornfield, where the dirt may be easily mounded. You'll need to construct a mound of soil, eighteen to twenty-four inches high, and at least two feet in diameter at the top. Drive a trap stake with a two-foot trap chain at the center of the area where you'll place your mound. While piling soil, keep the trap chain taut upward, so that in the end, the chain will be in the center of the mound, at the top, to attach your trap. As you build the mound, firm the soil around the base and sides, and finally flatten the top by tamping the soil with a shovel. Leave it slightly mounded, to shed water.

Dig out an area two inches bigger than the footprint of your trap on the top of the mound, about two inches deep. Coil the trap chain at the base of this hole and backfill until hole is one-inch deep. Place your trap in the hole, level the base of the dugout area, and tamp the soil firm. Carefully place the pre-set trap on the tamped area of the trap bed. Using your gloved hands, firm up the dirt tightly around the outside of the trap, preventing the trap from shifting or moving within the trap bed. At this point, cover the pan with the pan cloth or cover, making sure that the tear in the cloth is properly aligned with the trigger. Cover the trap with loose, sifted dirt, and brush to blend in the site.

Place a corn cob, rotted stick, cattail, or other natural material into the edge of the mound, and apply a few drops of fox urine. Place the attractor ten to twenty feet, downhill if possible, away from the constructed mound.

The Hay Bale Set

Foxes absolutely love to use hay bales as vantage points and as scent posts (read: defecating and urinating on the top of the hay bale). Mice frequently use the underside of hay bales as nesting sites, and as the fox is predominately a mouser, foxes are attracted to the hay bale as a food source. The trapper can use this to his or her advantage by placing a set at a hay bale. The set may be made on the top of the bale, or at one of the lower corners; both types are effective. Please note that we're discussing a square bale, which is much lower and smaller than a round bale.

Fox scat on an old hay bale, a perfect place for a set.

Don't try this method on the taller round bales, as it is impractical.

Top of The Bale

Look for a bale of hay with fox scat on or around it, or other evidence of fox activity, such as a dug-out mouse nest, tracks around the bale, and so on. Cut out a trap-size area with a knife in the top of the bale, about one inch deep. Using a long trap chain, anchor the trap to a stake, which is to be placed in the ground under the bale. Conceal your trap chain through the bale. Set the trap in the cut-out area and cover it with the material you have just removed from the top of the bale. Blend that material as best as possible, to conceal your trap. If you found any fox scat on top of the hay bale, carefully replace it four to six inches away from the edge of the trap. Squirt a small amount of fox urine on those droppings. On one corner of the bale, place a few drops of good gland lure, and a squirt or two of fox urine. This set is especially convenient and productive in the winter, with a light amount of snow cover.

Corner of the bale

This idea uses the fox's naturally inquisitive nature, and tendency to urinate on the corner of a hay bale, to trap him. At one corner of the hay bale, place and bed a trap four to six inches from the bale, in the same manner as described in the dirt hole set. Conceal and blend the trap with any natural material surrounding the site, or even use some ground-up hay from the bale itself. Place five or six drops of gland lure on the corner of the bale nearest the trap, taking great care not to get any lure on the trap or trap bed. On that same corner of the bale, place four or five squirts of fox urine.

In those fields that exhibit large amounts of fox activity, and more than one bale of hay, you can actually use both of these sets simultaneously (although on different hay bales), as I've often caught multiple foxes on the same night.

The Spring or Water Set

This is a very old trapping method, dating back to the nineteenth century, as it uses water to defeat the fox's ability to smell the trap, and yet takes full advantage of the fox's nature. Foxes will avoid getting their feet wet if they don't have to—much like a common house cat—and will use natural dry areas such as exposed stones, logs, or grass tussocks to traverse the wet areas. The principle is to use a situation where the fox is compelled to investigate a spot in a shallow wet area—a spring of water is a perfect example—and then create a stepping stone for the fox to use. It is on that stepping stone that your trap will be placed, and will use the fox's nature against him.

A spring is absolutely perfect because the water rarely freezes, and hardly ever rises or falls, as you're not dealing with runoff. The spring should be no more than four to six-feet in diameter, and if oblong, no more than four-feet wide at the widest point. You're looking for a shallow area, with the water no more than four-inches deep, surrounded by a flat area so the fox can approach on generally level ground. Within this spring of water, we will create the scenario which will bring, and ultimately trap, the fox.

I like to make my set while standing in the water source, as it will not transmit any scent to the area. On the bank of the spring, against the water's edge, place a flat rock about eight to ten inches in diameter so that it is level and one-half to three quarters of an inch above the water level. This will act as a natural approach to the set, and the fox will not hesitate to use it. Next, place the stepping/trap stone in such a

A perfect spot for the spring set.

manner that when the trap is placed on top of this stone, the trap jaw will be within one inch of the first stone you've placed, and deep enough so that a No. 2 double-coil spring trap will be one-quarter inch below the water's surface when placed on top of this rock. The trap should have a trap chain attached to a grapple or secured to a large drag, such as a log or stone. Conceal the trap chain and grapple/drag with mud and muck from the bottom of the water source.

The trap tension for this set should be approximately one pound (as opposed to the traditional eight ounces for other fox sets) as we'll be covering the trap with material (described momentarily), but you most definitely want this trap set to a hair trigger. The trap will be placed directly on the flat trap stone, again, so that the trap is covered by one-quarter inch of water. For covering material, you can use a pre-cut tight sod—found in lawns or cattle pastures—or the heavy, thick moss found growing on logs, stones, and rock faces in the woods, which I prefer. I harvest these whenever the opportunity arises, and I store in sealable plastic bags. Cut the sod/moss to fit perfectly inside the jaws of your trap. Carefully cover the trap pan with the sod/moss, placing it so only the sod or moss protrudes about one inch out of the water and so that the loose jaw faces the shore, one inch or less from the edge of the approach stone.

Now for the bait/lure stone, which is what will draw the fox to this set. Use any stone that will protrude an inch or more above the water line. Place it so there is gap of no more than two inches between the edge of the bait stone and the visible portion of the trap/stepping stone. This bait stone can be baited with a dead mouse, a piece of muskrat carcass, fresh fish, tainted venison, or other meat source that will naturally attract a fox. Cover this bait with grass or leaves—to conceal it from scavenger birds—and place a few drops of muskrat gland lure or a fox food lure on the bait and covering. Your bait and covering should protrude three to four inches above the water line when finished. When leaving the site, use the natural waterway as an exit to wash away your scent, just as you entered it. When checking the set, approach no closer than necessary to avoid scent contamination;

I use a binocular to check my set from a healthy distance.

The Scent Post

If you've ever walked a dog, you're familiar with the manner in which it prefers to urinate on or near an object, especially where another dog has urinated, as a means of marking territory. Foxes are no different, and the trapper can use that to his or her advantage. A scent post replicating something upon which a fox has previously urinated will draw in both male and female foxes, as their territoriality, instinct, and inquisitive nature will certainly get the better of them.

You'll want a flat area—avoid side hills—for this set, as it will best allow the fox to circle the set and comfortably investigate the area. This set will require a 'backing,' an object of attention—a corn cob, old bone, dried cow patty, or horse manure, fist-sized stone (no larger than a grapefruit), or small section of rotted log—to replicate a scenario where a fox has previously urinated. If using a small piece of wood, corn cob, or bone, stick it in the ground at a 30-degree angle, making it easier for the male fox to lift his leg and urinate. If using a stone, dried cow patty, or dried horse manure, it will obviously need to be placed flat on the ground.

Place your trap in the same fashion as described in the dirt hole set, with the pan of the trap located six to seven inches from the base of the backing or post. Using local material, such as sifted, dry grass, or crumbled, rotted cow patty or horse manure rubbed through your sifter, blend the trap as best you can into the local surroundings. If a post is used (bone, log, etc.), place a strong gland lure on the object, no lower than six inches above the ground, smearing it all over the object. At the base of the vertical post or bone, squirt a generous amount of fox urine. If using a stone, chunk of rotted wood, or cow patty—all of which will lay on the ground—use more urine than gland lure, placing just a drop or two of the gland lure on top of the object, and a liberal amount of fox urine at the base of the object.

For both sets, it's best to use a call lure, three to five feet away from the set, eighteen inches to two

A red fox is a very curious, yet wary animal. (Photo Credit: Getty Images.)

feet above the ground. If there is no natural object such as a branch or weeds, you can cut a stick and place the call lure on a cotton ball attached to the stick with a twist-tie or string. This will draw the fox into the general area much easier than relying on the urine scent alone. The fox will invariably investigate the area, and you'll have it in the trap.

This type of set may also be used in conjunction with a dirt hole set—keeping ten to twenty feet of separation between the two—and this combination has been known to catch two foxes in the same evening.

A Quick Set

This is a variation of the dirt hole set, but takes much less time to prepare. I've had the best success with this set in harvested cornfields, where the bases of the stalks remain in the field. The method of placing and bedding the trap is the same as described in the dirt hole set, but you'll punch a two-inch-diameter hole in the soil, six to seven inches away from the trap pan, straight down into the soil. Make the vertical hole four to six inches deep, placing a small bed of grass, or even better an old mouse nest, at the bottom, a food lure just above that, and cap it off with another bed of grass or mouse nest. Use a small round fist size stone or short two-inch-diameter stick on the opposite side of the hole where the trap is. Place a call lure on a stick located three to four feet away, and again eighteen to twenty-four inches off the ground.

This set is fast, yet effective, allowing the trapper to cover a lot of ground quickly. Foxes love these harvested cornfields for the mice that inhabit them, and this set has produced very well for me.

Snow/Frozen Ground Fox Sets

When trapping in freezing and/or snow cover conditions, line your trap bed and cover your traps with waxed dirt. I feel it works much better than waxed paper or peat moss. Detailed instructions on how to make your waxed dirt is covered elsewhere in this book (see chapter on coyotes).

When snow is on the ground and here to stay for the season, it much more difficult to set dirt hole and flat sets. Location becomes the thing that can make or break these sets. I am always on the lookout for windswept areas that are snow free—sometimes under a large cedar tree or at the top of a small hill. These spots are good places to construct a dirt hole set or flat set without leaving any sign of your being there. You basically construct your sets as normal, but use waxed dirt to bed and cover your traps, just as you would when constructing traps in normal non-freezing conditions. Always enter the snow-free area from the opposite side in which you intend to place your set.

Large Bait Set for Foxes

Foxes will regularly feed on large baits, especially when other prey is hard to come by in winter. I only use this set for foxes when at least four-plus inches of snow cover present. The large bait set method is covered extensively in the coyote section in this book. The only difference between setting for foxes and setting for coyotes is the distance between the traps (and I highly recommend using two traps).

For foxes I usually only leave a one-inch gap between the ends of the traps, and maybe not cover the traps with snow as deep. As for trap sizes for foxes at this set, I still use a No.3 or No. 2 coil spring, no smaller. I recommend using chains and grapples or drags instead of stakes. You can easily track up your catch in the snow.

This gray fox fell victim to a quick set.

Coyote—The Barking Dog

The coyote—*canis latrans*—is native to North America. It can be found from Central America to Alaska, from the Atlantic Ocean to the Pacific Ocean. There are about nineteen subspecies of coyotes. They vary greatly in size and color, depending on their geographic location. The males will range between eighteen and forty-four pounds on average, and females run fifteen to forty pounds on average. They will measure three to four feet long from nose to tail, with a fourteen- to eighteen-inch bushy tail. As a general rule, the farther north you go, the larger the coyote. Here in the Northeast, it is not uncommon to take a large male weighing over fifty pounds.

Coyotes have some wolf DNA in them; I have read that the northeastern coyotes also have some domestic dog DNA. As for color, the coyotes found in colder climates are mostly black and gray with a

The eastern coyote, larger than his western cousin. (Photo Credit: Getty Images.)

little dark brown. Here in upstate New York, most are dark, but I have observed a few that appeared to be almost blonde. The coyotes in warmer climates are more whitish, made up of gray and tan.

Albinos are very rare. Coyotes have a soft, thick underfur with long, coarse guard hairs. Their natural enemies are humans, followed by wolves and cougars. They are good swimmers, and will travel over long distances over ice. When I was hunting moose

A coyote on the lighter side of the color spectrum.

in Newfoundland, the guide was talking about how they now see coyotes, which they had never had on the island. I asked who brought them here. His reply was, "Nobody." He told me that they walked across on the ice from the mainland.

Coyotes breed in mid-winter and have a litter of about five to six pups, each weighing a half-pound to a full pound, after a sixty-three-day gestation period. Once paired up, and mated—a process which can take up to two months of courtship—the male is strictly monogamous, and helps raise and feed his pups. In fact, while his mate is pregnant, he does most of his hunting alone and brings back food to his mate. She is busy cleaning out their den—which can be a hollow tree or log or a cleaned-out burrow of another animal—and lining it with leaves and other soft matter. They sometimes use the same den for consecutive years. Their pups are born blind and are dependent strictly on milk alone for the first ten to twelve days. Their eyes open about the tenth day. They will start to eat some solid food at about two weeks of age,

usually regurgitated food from their parents. This lasts until the pups are about five weeks old and then they can eat the pieces of prey that their parents present to them. The pups leave the den about mid-June and travel with the parents. It is not unheard of that related, un-bred females help in the raising of the pups. The pups are full grown in about nine months. If you wonder if there is a litter of young coyotes in your area, just listen when the noon whistle or siren sounds, and you will hear the whole litter answering in a high pitched howl.

Coyotes mostly travel in related packs; unrelated packs are usually made up of bachelor males. The coyote's diet consists of 90 percent meat, the rest being made up of fruits, vegetables, insects, and grasses. Their wild prey varies largely, being deer, fawns, rabbits, mice, fish, frogs, snakes, woodchucks, muskrats, and any other animal they can easily take, being the opportunists that they are. They mostly hunt the smaller ones like mice and rabbits alone, but attack the larger ones like full-grown deer, goats, and sheep

A handsome male coyote. (Photo Credit: Getty Images.)

in packs of two or more. Being opportunists, they regularly prey on domestic stock, like sheep and their lambs, calves, goats, domestic fowl, small dogs, and cats. They have also been known to attack humans, but these attacks are rare, and mostly in California, for one reason or another. It has been estimated that a single coyote eats about 550 pounds of food a year. The coyote's territory can be as great as twenty-four square miles, depending on populations and food availability. They are normally very human shy, but at the same time live in close proximity to human activity. Believe it or not, there are coyotes living and thriving inside New York City—not in large numbers, but nevertheless, they are there.

The coyote will cache its unused food and sometimes urinates on it, I suppose as a means of claiming to the rest of the world. This is the basic premise that the dirt hole set works on. Coyotes travel over paths, game trails, and logging roads, as well as just

going straight where they have a mind to go. They can travel three to ten miles per day. They are active twenty-four hours a day, but are much more active at night. For a long time I was under the impression that their olfactory ability (sense of smell) was the most important sense they used when hunting. Studies have proven sight is first and foremost, however, with smell and hearing coming in close behind. Coyotes have been known to peaceably interact with badgers, and have even been witnessed digging for rodents together.

Traps

For coyotes, the smallest size trap I recommend is a #2 four-coil. The first coyote that I ever caught (for a brief time) was at my fox set. I had used a #2 double-coil spring at that time because it was the largest trap I had, and I did not have enough money to buy any of the larger traps. At that point in time there were

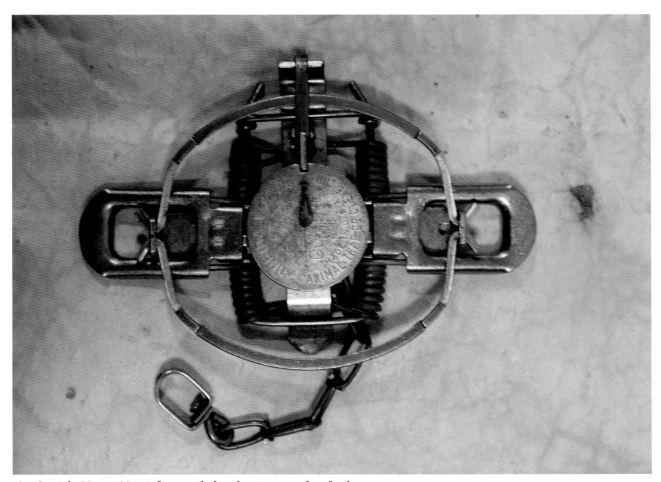

An Oneida Victor No. 3 four-coiled coil spring, perfect for large coyotes.

very few coyotes in my area and all my sets were for foxes. A landowner, who was a farmer, stopped me on my way to check my traps, and told me he could see at a distance that I had a coyote in my fox set, out at the back of his hay lot. When I walked closer I did not see any sign of the coyote. Upon inspecting the empty set I observed the coyote had pulled so hard on the trap that it unhinged the jaws and escaped. Lesson learned! If the farmer did not see the coyote at the set from his barn, I would have never known what had happened for sure.

There are some very large coyotes here in upstate New York. A #3 coil or even #4 (if it is legal in your state) would have been a much better choice, especially with snow conditions. It is best to avoid using double-long spring traps, as these types of traps are larger and heavier to carry, and take up an excessive amount of room in the trap bed. But if they are all you have, try to make the best with what you have to work with.

I prep and tune my traps in the same manner as stated in the section on trapping foxes. I do cut down the size of the pans on some of my traps, but not all. I use these traps with the pan size slightly smaller, mostly for my dirt hole sets. It gives me a little more assurance of a good, solid catch. All traps have at least three swivels and if the chain is extra long, it will have probably four swivels. When trapping coyotes you have to be just as concerned with being scent-free as when fox trapping, and maybe even more.

Trap Staking

Coyotes are much more powerful than foxes. If using steel trap stakes, as described in the fox trapping section, they should be even longer—preferably one-half- or five-eighths-inch reinforcing bars—of twenty-four to thirty inches in length, and prepared the same way as fox stakes. The stake should be sharpened to a point on one end and have a nut or washer welded to the other (I prefer it one-quarter- to one-half inch below the top, so the nut/washer and weld aren't hit by the hammer when setting the stake), to attach the trap chain. Just below the nut or washer I grind off an inch or two of the distressed portion of the rebar to allow the lap link or quick link at the end of the chain to swivel freely, with no resistance. Your stakes should be dyed and waxed in the same manner as your traps.

I have been getting away from anchoring my coyotes sets with stakes, as I now try to use a long chain and grapple when there is enough vegetation nearby to entangle the coyote. When using grapples on coyotes, the longer trap chains work much better; I personally use a six-foot-long chain. Where the situation is not advantageous for a grapple, like a set in a very large hay lot or open field, or when you do not have a lot of time to spend looking for your catch, I will use an earth anchor and cable. They cost about two dollars each when purchased with cable already attached. They are available in different length of cables and different widths for use in different soil conditions. You simply attach your trap to the end of the cable and you're done. They are much lighter to carry and drive into the soil very fast. I highly recommend using these for coyotes.

Lures and Bait

There is an uncountable amount of lures and baits on the market today, and most work very well. Some will work well for one trapper, while the same lure and bait will have poor results for another. Through trial and error, you will find what works best for you in your area at different sets, and the same applies to baits. A trapper friend of mine, who did very well with coyotes, used nothing but a gland lure, some coyote droppings, and coyote urine for all his sets. What I use at dirt hole sets is a combination of everything, mixing it up at each set. Some sets I use with bait, lure, and urine, some sets just bait and urine, some sets with just lure and urine, and some with just gland lure and bait. I used to buy my baits, but now make my own. I still purchase my gland lures, brands that are from proven manufacturers that have been on the market for many years. The same applies to urine. They have worked well for me, so if it is not broke, don't fix it. When you finally find a lure or bait that works well, keep this information to yourself. You don't want your competition using it and, even much worse than that, a sloppy trapper educating every coyote in your area. In this chapter I will share with you a coyote bait recipe that you can make yourself, that has worked very well for me.

Coyote and Fox Bait Recipe

It is pretty much settled research that all canines respond best to a fatty acid scent (tainted meat). This, in my opinion, is the basics for any good bait for foxes and coyotes. Different meats give off different smells. To humans, most tainted meats smell alike, but to a canine each one is different. Their sense of smell is many, many times more sensitive than that of humans. Their survival depends on it. These animals do not smell things as humans do. We humans smell things as a whole food. For example, a good beef stew has a smell we all can recognize. We smell it and we say, beef stew. A coyote smells in parts or layers. If a coyote smelled the same beef stew, a coyote will smell the meat, the potatoes, the carrots, and all the other ingredients in the stew separately. The same applies to the bait you use. The coyote will smell all the ingredients in your bait separately, not the smell or scent of the bait as a whole. Knowing this, you now realize the importance of each and every component you mix into your bait.

If you used only one ingredient in your bait, the coyote might not be interested enough to work the set. You have not created a complex enough scent mixture to draw him in and make him work the set. If it were easy, just a plain piece of meat would work every time. There are so many baits on the market today, using hundreds of different concoctions and ingredients stating that they are the best bait available. Most will draw coyotes in and work well and some not so well. The following recipe is very basic, will work for most coyotes, and will work in warm and cold conditions. Meat is the base ingredient. I like to use a combination of natural meats that the coyote preys upon in the wild. These include rabbit, muskrat, venison, woodchuck, and skunk. I usually pick equal parts of any three or four on the list but always include muskrat as one of them. I clean,

debone, and grind them into ground meat. If using three, I use a third of a pound of each, as the goal is to end up with about a pound of ground meat in total. If you choose to use four different meats, use a quarter pound of each. The glands of the muskrats are ground into the muskrat meat as well, and if I have any extra glands I add them also. Another item I add anytime I have it is the stomach fat from a coyote. I put each meat in a separate container to taint for about five days. Place a cheese cloth over the top of each jar and lightly screw the lid on, allowing gases to escape and not allowing any flies access to the contents. Place the jars in a warm place and cover them with a bucket for extra protection from flies and the like.

Coyotes are voracious predators.

The meats should be well tainted after five days. Combine all the meats and blend together. Now add three tablespoons of melted lanolin and three ounces of vegetable oil and mix well into the tainted ground meats. Next, blend in a tablespoon of beaver castor. When you have thoroughly blended all the ingredients together, add three tablespoons of sodium benzoate, stirring so every part of the bait is exposed to the sodium benzoate. The last ingredient is glycerin; this will keep the meat from freezing solid in cold weather. Add in about four ounces and again mix thoroughly. Place the finished bait into a clean glass jar with a tight lid, and check in twenty-four hours to make sure there are no gases building. If you find gases are building in the jar, you need to add more sodium benzoate to the bait. I like to make this bait in one-pound servings. If I want more than one batch, I make it all over from scratch, and mix up the meats used. This way it never comes out exactly the same and offers the coyote a variety of appealing smells.

The way I usually use this bait is to place about a tablespoon down the dirt hole on a small grass plug or small piece of rabbit fur or sheep's wool. Cover the bait with a loose grass plug. Use urine and gland lure as you always do. If using this bait for a flat set, I place it on a grass plug, under a tufted of grass or small piece of rotten wood. If trapping in very cold and freezing conditions, or if you want to offer a slightly different smell, you can add five to ten drops of tincture of skunk to the batch.

Trap Sets for Coyotes

The Dirt Hole Set

The dirt hole set is one of the most popular sets used for trapping coyotes. In my opinion, coyotes work these sets for a number of reasons; sometimes to steal another animal's cache, sometimes just for an easy meal, and sometimes just out of curiosity. It is the combination of all three that you want present at the dirt hole set. Coyotes are opportunists, and will continually rob the cache of another animal. If not done correctly, the dirt hole set will quickly educate every coyote that comes in contact with your set. This is one of the main reasons for "mixing it up" and not making every set the same in looks and smell.

Many well-made baits and lures have become ineffective by improperly made sets and applications. This goes for every kind of set you make for coyotes. Like in real estate, one of the most important parts of a dirt hole set is location. Preseason scouting and always looking for sign while working your trap line plays a large part.

Coyotes love the edges of large fields, cultivated or not, and especially love the points of hedgerows and woods, the same as foxes do. If there are ponds in the area, the dykes are a place where coyotes will visit,

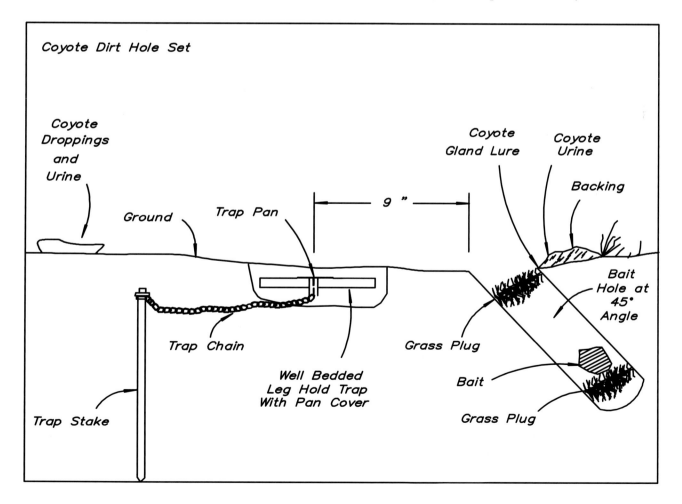

Coyote Dirt Hole Set

Coyote Droppings and Urine

Coyote Gland Lure

Coyote Urine

Backing

Ground

Trap Pan

9"

Bait Hole at 45° Angle

Trap Chain

Grass Plug

Bait

Well Bedded Leg Hold Trap With Pan Cover

Grass Plug

Trap Stake

looking for mice and muskrats. Coyotes and foxes seem to frequent the same areas, such as the edges of hay lots where farmers have abandoned old hay bales, as they hold a prolific amount of mice. A large clearing in the woods can also be a good choice for a dirt hole, providing the soil conditions are favorable, and not subject to flooding. Any set for a coyote must be such as to keep fear and suspicion to an absolute minimum.

Look for a natural open spot at least thirty feet in diameter, free of logs, underbrush, bushes, and taller grass, with an area that will drain away from your set. If need be, remove any of the above objects; some trappers prefer to mow the area with a small machete, scythe, or even a push lawn mower, before season to make the area as natural as possible for the coyote.

With your exact set location determined, you can now proceed, following these step-by-step set instructions.

Always wearing clean rubber gloves to handle traps and tools, set your trap before you even approach the site. Always approach the set from downwind, the breeze in your face. Now place your drop cloth so you can kneel without leaving any scent. If you're using rubber hip boots, be sure they cover your knees if you're not using the drop cloth to kneel on. Your drop cloth—whether it's being knelt upon or simply used to keep your equipment from contacting the ground—should always be placed with the same side touching the ground, and that side folded in when leaving the set to keep the drop cloth as scent-free as possible. A small plastic bucket can be used to carry all the necessary equipment to the set instead of the entire trap basket. Plastic buckets are much easier to keep scent-free, and can be washed out much easier. I keep this bucket within arm's length, on the drop cloth, for easy access. Once in position, stay there until the set is complete.

Using a hoe, clear out and scrape an egg-shaped to tear-drop-shaped oval site, some measuring one-and one-half feet wide by two feet long, with some just large enough to fit my bedded trap and every size in-between. Remove all sod and clumps of vegetation. This will house both the trap and the bait hole.

Place the removed sod and vegetation on the drop cloth for future use and/or removal. At the pointed end of the site, as close to a 45-degree angle to the ground as possible, dig the bait hole. The exact size and shape of the hole can vary from two inches in diameter to six inches in diameter. The depth, in my opinion, should be nine to twelve inches deep. This will be your bait hole. The dirt removed from the bait hole should be placed in the sifter for future use.

Next thing you need to do is to scrape out the trap bed, the center of which should be nine inches from the edge of the bait hole and roughly two inches deeper than the level of the finished set. The trap bed needs to be slightly larger than the footprint of your chosen trap. Tamp the trap bed with a stone or small hammer until the ground is firm. At this time, drive the trap stake or anchor with trap attached. Replace three-quarter inches of loose, stone-free dirt into the trap bed. Carefully place the trap into the loose dirt of the trap bed, with the center of the trap pan nine inches out from the edge of the bait hole and three inches to the right offset from center. Place the trap so the dog is pointing to the left and not at the bait hole. This will result with the coyote stepping between the jaws and not over the jaws. Using your gloved hands, firm up the dirt tightly around the outside of the trap, preventing the trap from shifting or moving within the trap bed. This is VERY IMPORTANT; you do not want the trap to move the least little bit when pressure is applied anywhere on the trap, epically the jaws. At this point, cover the pan with the pan cover of choice, making sure that the tear in the cover is properly aligned with the trigger. Using the dirt previously placed in the sifter, sift this soil over the entire trap bed to blend in the bed with the site, constantly packing the dirt around the trap to stabilize it leaving no rises or depressions. The only soft spot should be over the pan. With a small branch, or brush—I prefer a pine bough—brush the entire trap bed to make it look natural.

Next we must bait and lure the set. First I place a grass plug at the bottom of the hole. For the next step, you must remove your gloves and place them back in the bucket or basket (I use a gallon-size sealable freezer bag to store my gloves) as you do not want bait or lure scent or any other foreign odors on your gloves. Using the bait fork, large spoon, or sharpened stick, place a walnut- to egg-sized piece of bait at the back of the bait hole. Cover the bait with a small amount of dirt, or as I prefer, a plug of dead grass, if available. Place six to ten drops of gland lure at the top edge of the bait hole, allowing some to fall onto the grass plug or cover dirt. One piece of bait should be enough, as our goal is to entice the coyote to work the set, not to fatten him up.

Using your spray bottle filled with coyote urine, spray a mist over the entire set, concentrating a few squirts into the bait hole. Though optional, I have noticed that using dead grass and dry leaves sifted through the grater, then covering the entire set with finely grated grass, will not only break up the pattern, but will entice those coyotes which have been previously educated to the dirt hole set to maybe give it another try. A few coyote droppings that have been given a squirt of fresh urine, placed at the back edge of the set about twelve inches from the center of the trap, can be a good suspicion remover.

A call lure can be used to entice coyotes from long distances. Place an absorbent article—a corn cob, a mouse's nest, a piece of boiled cloth, a large cotton ball, etc.—approximately twenty feet away from and upwind of the prevailing wind direction at a height of four feet above the ground. Apply ten drops of a good call lure (purchased from a trapping supply company) to the article, to allow the scent to disperse and bring the coyote close enough to investigate the dirt hole set.

At this point, I'd to share some subtleties that can make a significant difference in success. Regarding trap placement, I've learned the hard way that if using a trap placement position that requires the coyote to step over the jaw, as opposed to in-between the jaws, place the triggered jaw toward the bait hole. This prevents the coyote from stepping on the trigger and pan simultaneously, which can push his paw upward and out of the trap as the trigger flies up to release the jaw. It's happened to me numerous times before someone educated me, and I hope it prevents you from having to learn the hard way.

Another common mistake is placing the trap too close to the bait hole. It's better to have the trap farther away than to be too close.

I've also learned to dress up and vary my dirt hole sets by placing coyote droppings, previously collected while scouting, on the outside edge of the dirt hole pattern, and giving it a quick squirt of coyote urine, as a visual and olfactory attractor and as a suspicion remover.

I've adorned my bait hole plug with small bird feathers, in an attempt to recreate a situation where a coyote has taken a bird. I've also used rabbit and deer fur, or other small pieces of natural fur, such as a squirrel tail, to add variety to my dirt hole sets. Be careful not to overdo this as it will attract crows and other scavenging birds that will set off your set. If four days go by with no activity, I re-spray the site with coyote urine to keep it smelling good. I'll reapply my gland lure every eight or nine days, possibly more frequently if it's been raining.

Hopefully, you'll have caught a coyote before you need to freshen up the set, and you'll need to rebuild your set after a catch. Once you've dispatched the coyote you've trapped, you'll see a torn-up circle where the animal worked to escape, but was restrained by the trap, chain, and stake or anchor. After dispatching the coyote, remove the coyote from area immediately and carefully inspect the torn-up area and remove any and all—no matter how small—drops or clots of blood. The presence of decomposed blood in your set will prompt another visiting animal to dig and roll in the bloodied area, which will result in springing the trap, only catching hair. Use the trowel to dig underneath any blood-soaked soil, and cast that soil away from your set. Remove any dirt within the site which has been contaminated with bait, lure, or blood. This will include cleaning the surface of the bait hole, and covering the bait again; the bait may be reused in the hole, though you may want to freshen it. Re-level the soil at the site with your hoe, and if you plan to reuse the same trap, remove all blood and hair from the entire trap with a coyote urine–soaked rag. I personally would rather use a new clean trap, and put the used trap in a gallon freezer bag, so I can clean and re-wax it at home. Utilizing the original bait hole if possible, prepare the site as described above. Place bait back in the hole, but you'll need a few fresh drops of gland lure, as the previous catch will have dispersed its natural scents. Any droppings that resulted from the catch can be placed on the edge of the pattern, as a natural attractant.

If you trap a species other than coyote or fox in this set, I would recommend you abandon the site, starting over a few yards away. The former site will be a general attractor, but the new dirt hole will not smell of other animals.

There are a few variations to the dirt hole that I feel you should know about. They are two- and even three-hole dirt hole sets. You construct your dirt hole as instructed above, but you add an additional smaller hole three inches to the right or left of the main hole. I normally put the additional hole to the same side I have offset the trap pan to.

The bait hole is the larger hole, and in the smaller hole I place a gland lure and some urine. For the three-hole set I place two smaller holes each three inches either side of the main larger bait hole and a few inches closer to the trap. In one I place urine, in the other I place a gland lure, and bait in the main larger hole. These smaller holes can be as small as one inch in diameter. Another thing worth mentioning is that if I have the traps available, I sometimes set an additional trap, bedded as usual about thirty inches out from the main trap. It is a blind set, with no lure, bait, or urine. This is not to catch an additional coyote, but rather to catch the coyote in two traps to ensure no escape, or just catch him approaching the set while he is focused on the attractant.

The Mound Set

This set is one of the easiest sets to construct, catches those coyotes that have been educated to the hole sets, and catches very few non-target animals, including dogs and cats. It uses the coyote's natural inquisitiveness, curiosity, and instincts to investigate an attractant, from a higher perch, to the trapper's advantage. Coyotes as well as foxes simply love to use small mounds or humps to gain a visual advantage when investigating that which they find interesting. I prefer to use a natural attractant such as a half-buried skunk or rabbit, a deer tail or portion of a leg (especially a back leg with hock gland intact), a muskrat carcass, or a squirrel, all except the skunk or deer leg with some call lure on it. The principle is to have the coyote circle the attractant, and ultimately use the mound for a visual advantage, where it will be caught in your trap.

Ant hills are a good choice, if large enough, as their natural condition offers excellent drainage, they are usually scent-free, and the soil will not freeze. Ant hill soil is prized by fox trappers, and is often harvested and kept for use in other sets, especially in wet and cold conditions. Find an ant hill no higher than eighteen inches tall and eighteen to twenty-four inches in diameter or larger at the top, the bigger the better for this coyote set. If no ant hills are in the area, you can construct your own mound, or take advantage of other natural formations such as rotted stumps. Open areas, like cattle pastures, hay lots, or even on the edges of harvested grain fields are good places to look for these mounds or ant hills. A large clearing in the woods, where old stumps have rotted, is also a good location for this set. What you're looking for is an area with a 360-degree view for at least twenty feet, preferably more.

Stake Method, on an Ant Hill

Dig out an area two inches bigger than the footprint of your trap; I prefer a No. 2 four-coil spring or a No. 3 coil spring for this set. On the top of the mound, about five inches deep, and save that precious material for future use. You'll need a trap stake two feet in length or longer, and drive it down in the center of the hill, as far as possible. Attach your trap with three-foot-long trap chain, and possibly a bit longer, as you want the coyote to be pulling perpendicular to the axis of the trap stake rather than straight up, once caught. Coil the trap chain on top of the stake, at the bottom of the five-inch-deep area, and

The No. 3 four-coiled offset jaw trap is perfect for the ant hill coyote set.

backfill with soil until within an inch of the top of the mound. Tamp and level the base of the dug-out area, and tamp the soil firm. Carefully place the pre-set trap on the tamped area of the trap bed. Using your gloved hands, firm up the previously collected ant hill dirt tightly around the outside of the trap, preventing the trap from shifting or moving within the trap bed. At this point, cover the pan with the pan cloth or cover, making sure that the tear in the cloth is properly aligned with the trigger. Re-tamp the dirt around the trap. Using your sifter, cover the trap with sifted dirt which you removed from the mound, to make it equal to or slightly higher than the original height of the mound. Smooth and grade this loose material with a pine bough or small broom to blend it in. On the edge of the ant hill, place a couple dozen drops of coyote urine. Place your attractor ten to thirty feet away so the there is an unobstructed view between the mound and the attractor. Again, it's a simple concept, but very effective, especially in frigid temperatures when others fail.

Drag Method, on an Ant Hill

This is very similar to the method described above, except your trap hole is only two inches deep instead of five, as we'll be wiring the trap chain to a drag instead of using a stake. Take a length of clean No. 9 wire or heavier, and push it down the center of your trap bed at a 45-degree angle until it exits the side of the base of the ant hill. Attach one end of the wire to your trap chain and the other end of this wire firmly to the center of a four- to five-foot-long, four-inch-diameter log, to serve as a drag. Pull on the drag end of the wire until the end of the trap chain is firm against the trap bed at the top of the ant hill. Cover the wire and drag with local material and blend in. Bed and cover trap in the same manner previously described above, using urine and attractor in the same manner.

The Constructed Mound

This method works best in a cultivated field, such as a harvested cornfield, where the dirt may be easily mounded. You'll need to construct a mound of soil, eighteen to twenty-four inches high, and at least four feet in diameter at the bottom and eighteen to twenty-four inches at the top. Drive a trap stake or place a drag or grapple with a two- to three-foot trap chain at the center of the area where you'll place your mound. If using a grapple, the chain can be longer; just coil it up on the ground. While piling soil, keep the trap chain taut upward, so that in the end the chain will be in the center at the top of the finished mound, to attach your trap to. As you build the mound, firm the soil around the base and sides, and finally flatten the top by tamping the soil with a shovel. Leave it slightly mounded, to shed water.

Dig out an area two inches larger than the footprint of your trap on the top of the mound, and about two inches deep. Coil the trap chain at the bottom of this hole, backfill, and tamp until the hole is one inch deep. Place your trap in the hole, level the base of the dug-out area, and tamp the soil firm again. Carefully place the pre-set trap on the tamped area of the trap bed. Using your gloved hands, firm up the dirt tightly around the outside of the trap, preventing the trap from shifting or moving within the trap bed. At this point, cover the pan with the pan cloth or cover, making sure that the tear in the cloth is properly aligned with the trigger. Cover the trap with loose, sifted dirt, and brush to blend in the site.

Place a corn cob, rotted stick, small cattail, small bleached bone, or other natural material into the edge of the mound, and apply a few drops of coyote urine. If you have them, you can also place a few urine-sprayed coyote droppings on top of one edge of the mound instead of the previous mentioned items. Place the attractor ten to twenty feet, downhill if possible, away from the constructed mound.

The Hay Bale Set

Coyotes, as well as foxes, absolutely love to use hay bales as vantage points and scent posts (read defecating and urinating on the top of the hay bale). Mice frequently use the undersides of hay bales as nesting sites, and as coyotes never will pass up a free meal, these are natural spots coyotes will frequent. The trapper can use this to his or her advantage by placing a set at a hay bale. The set may be made on the top of the bale, or at one of the lower corners; both types are effective. Please note that we're discussing a square bale, which is much lower and smaller than the large round bales. Don't try this method on the taller round bales, as it is impractical.

Top of the Bale

Look for a bale of hay with coyote or fox scat on or around it, or other evidence of coyote activity such as a dug-out mouse nest, tracks around the bale, and so on. Cut out a trap-size area with a knife in the top of the bale, about one inch deep. Using a long trap chain, anchor the trap to a stake, which is to be placed in the ground under the bale. Conceal your trap chain through the bale. Set the trap in the cut-out area, use a pan cover and cover it with the material you have just removed from the top of the bale, running it through your sifter until trap is completely canceled. You can shave off some from the sides of the bail if more material is needed. Blend that material as best as possible, to conceal your trap. If you found any coyote or fox scat on top of the hay bale, carefully replace it six to eight inches away from the edge of the trap. Squirt a small amount of coyote urine on those droppings. On one corner of the bale, place a few drops of good gland lure, and another squirt or two of coyote urine. This set is especially convenient and productive in the winter, with a light amount of snow cover in the forecast.

Corner of the Bale

This idea uses the coyote's tendency to urinate on the corner of a hay bale, and snoop around for a fresh mouse nest to plunder, as a means to trap him. At one corner of the hay bale, place and bed a trap so that the closest jaw is about six to nine inches from the bale, in the same manner as described in the dirt hole set. Conceal and blend the covered trap with any natural material surrounding the site, or even use some ground-up hay from the bale itself by running it through your sifter. Place five or six drops of gland lure on the corner of the bale nearest the trap, taking great care not to get any lure on the trap or trap bed. On that same corner of the bale, place four or five squirts of coyote urine.

In those fields that exhibit large amounts of coyote activity, and more than one bale of hay, you can actually use both of these sets simultaneously (although on different hay bales), as it is possible to catch multiple coyotes on the same night.

The Scent Post and Flat Sets

If you've ever walked a dog, you're familiar with the manner in which it prefers to urinate on or near an object where another dog or animal has urinated, for one reason or another. A scent post or flat set uses this habit to draw the coyote in to the set.

For this set you will want a flat area—avoid side hills—as it will best allow the coyote to circle and

approach the set without any difficulty. I usually pick a spot three to five feet off a trail or wood road frequently traveled by coyotes. This set will require a "backing," an object of attention, being a bleached old bone, dried cow patty or horse manure, an outstanding clump of grass, or small section of rotted log, to replicate a scenario where a coyote or fox has previously urinated. If using a small piece of wood, or bone, stick it in the ground at a 30-degree angle leaning away from the trap bed, making it more enticing for the male coyote to lift his leg and urinate. If using an outstanding clump of grass, dried cow patty, or dried horse manure, it will obviously need to be placed flat on the ground. You can place a very small branch on the opposite side away from the trap to force the coyote to use the trap side of the "scent post."

Place and bed your trap in the same fashion as described in the dirt hole set, with the pan of the trap located about eight inches from the base of the

Coyote scat along a trail in an open field.

backing or post. Using local material, such as sifted, dry grass, or crumbled, rotted cow patty or horse manure rubbed through your sifter, blend the covered trap as best you can into the local surroundings. If a post is used (bone, log, etc.), place a strong gland lure on the object, no lower than six inches above the ground, smearing it all over the object. At the base of the vertical post or bone, squirt a generous amount of coyote urine. If using a chunk of rotted wood or cow patty, all of which will lie on the ground, use more urine than gland lure, placing just a drop or two of the gland lure on top of the object, and a liberal amount of coyote urine at the base of the object.

For both sets, it's best to use a call lure, three to five feet away from the set, and eighteen inches to two feet above the ground. If there is no natural object such as a branch or weeds, you can cut a stick and place the call lure on a cotton ball attached to the stick with a twist-tie or string. This will act to draw the coyote into the general area much more effectively than relying merely on the urine scent alone. The coyote will invariably investigate the site.

This type of set may also be used in conjunction with a dirt hole set. Keeping twenty to thirty feet of separation between the dirt hole set and the scent post set, this combination has been known to catch two coyotes in the same night.

The Woodchuck Hole Set

In tracking coyotes while hunting, I have noticed that they seem to investigate woodchuck holes more often than not. I have noticed that they would go out of their way to check one out, and then turn 90 degrees and be back on their intended path again. I think one of the reasons—besides that they regularly prey upon woodchucks—is that chuck hunters shoot a lot of woodchucks while the woodchuck is standing right outside or next to its hole. A lot of chuck hunters never retrieve the chucks and if they even bother to go see for sure that they killed the chuck, after finding it they merely throw the dead chuck down its hole. Coyotes must be in the habit of checking these holes for free meals, even when the woodchucks have went in for the long sleep of

winter. This set is only practical when we are positive the woodchucks are in for the winter, as we do not want to catch woodchucks, just coyotes. When the chucks are asleep, the ground is usually frozen, so you will need some "waxed dirt" for this set. There are detailed instructions for preparing waxed dirt elsewhere in this book. What I do for the chuck hole set is use it like a dirt hole set. I always pick a chuck hole that is on a relatively flat area; avoid chuck holes that are in side hills. Coyotes still frequent them, but it is very hard to ensure a catch with this condition. I chop out a flat area for a trap bed and stake, large enough to conceal same at the mouth of the chuck hole, so that when completed the pan of the trap is nine to twelve inches out from the edge of the hole. If the chuck hole is at a very flat angle and not at 45 degrees to the surrounding ground, I will keep the pan at least twelve inches out or more. Try to pick chuck holes that go into the ground at 45 degrees or close to it. When my trap bed is complete, and the stake is installed, I line the bed with about one half to three-quarters of an inch of waxed dirt and pat it down so it is firm. (In this chapter there is a method of preparing your own waxed dirt.) Now bed the trap firmly in the waxed dirt and place more waxed dirt around the entire trap and pack it tightly around the trap so it will not move. Next place your pan cover over the pan and fill in the rest of the trap with more waxed dirt. Now fill in any areas left outside your waxed dirt with regular soil so that the trap bed with trap is relatively level. Using your sifter, cover the entire trap bed with waxed dirt, about three-eighths of an inch deep.

Place an egg-size amount of coyote bait about one foot down the chuck hole. You might have to place a grass plug down the hole first to stop the bait from going down the chuck hole further than one foot. About four or five feet away, place some call lure about three feet above the ground. Brush away any signs of your being there and exit the set.

The Double Step Set

This set is strictly a blind set, meaning that there is not any lure, bait, or urine involved. It relies entirely

Coyote tracks in soft soil.

on the coyote just traveling on a well-used and well-defined trail, whether it is a trail through the grass field, a crossing over a ditch between fields, or a wheel track on a farm road or logging road. I like to pick a well-drained spot on the trail, so no water will collect or puddle in my set. You must be sure that there will be no vehicular, off-road, or farm machinery traffic if using a wheel track. Coyote sign on the trail you use must be present and obvious. This set works well if set just before a light snow fall, but will work satisfactorily in dry weather. Once you have decided you have a well-used coyote trail, pick a level area on the trail higher than the surrounding parts of the trail so that no water will accumulate on your set, no low spots. You will bed two traps precisely in line with the trail. Traps should be set so the coyote steps between the jaws and not over them. For this set I do not use pan covers but rather a blocked pan: Placing soft material under the pan allows the trap to fire, but does not allow the underside of the pan to fill in with bedding material. This can be purchased from trapping supply stores or you can make one yourself. You can use the fluffy polyester filling from a modern non-down pillow. Do not use a pillow that has been used; buy a new one just for this purpose, as a used pillow is obviously full of human scent. Distance between the pans should be ten inches. I do not stake this set but prefer to use grapples. This makes it possible to reuse the same location after a catch. Also, it usually leaves one of the traps intact for another possible catch. I dig a small trench off to the side, about a foot long, to bury the trap chain and hide the rest of the chain off to

the side by covering it with local material. The traps must be bedded very tight with no movement at all. Cover traps with sifted, local material if non-freezing conditions exist. If there are freezing conditions, use waxed dirt to bed and cover the traps. After the traps are bedded and covered, the only soft spot at the set should be over the pans. Blend in with natural material so you cannot tell that there has been any disturbance to the trail.

Place a pencil-sized stick about eight inches long or a piece of coyote scat exactly halfway between the pans so that the coyote will naturally step over the stick or scat and into the trap. In my opinion, coil spring traps are much more suited for this set than long spring traps. If snow is on the ground, check the set with binoculars and approach no closer than necessary to check the set. After a catch, use a clean trap, as you do not want any odors, friendly or not, drawing attention to the set. If there is snow on the ground, I take a broom and smooth and blend out the snow fifty feet in both directions on the trail when I reset my traps after a catch. I also blend in my tracks as I move away from the area. Some trappers use a call lure twenty to thirty feet up or down the trail. I do not, as I want nothing there that might make coyotes veer off from their intended path. Always approach and exit your set from the side at right angles, especially with snow cover.

Trapping at Large Baits for Coyotes

This set is much more productive with snow cover than without; actually, I would not even attempt it without snow cover. A large bait source such as a dead deer, goat, sheep, cattle, etc.—the heavier the better—is an extremely great opportunity to take coyote in winter. You can place a large bait where you think it will be most advantageous for you or use an existing one placed by others or nature. If using smaller large bait, like goat, sheep, or deer, it is best to anchor it down to a tree or any other natural object. If you recently placed a large bait, it may take several days for the coyotes to find it and start feeding on it on a regular basis. Coyotes will frequent large baits for a free meal daily. In doing so, they usually will travel the same path or trail through the snow to the large bait. There may be several heavily used trails to the large bait coming in from different directions. Though it is tempting to just set a few traps at the large bait site, this may not produce any catch, let alone multiple catches over time. Once you have located the large bait source, or had placed one there beforehand just for this purpose, do not walk right to the bait to check for activity. The best way to check for activity is to walk a complete circle, keeping at least one hundred yards away at all times from the bait; one fifty would be better.

When you come across any trails that are heading to your bait, do not step in the trail, and remove as much evidence of your being there as possible. If there is not any activity going on at your bait, wait a week and check again. When you find a well-used trail going to or from or both ways from the bait, these are the trails you want to set your traps on. The trails which have tracks going in both directions are the ones I would use first. Traps should not be set any closer than seventy-five yards from the actual bait. Approach those trails you intend to place your traps on right angles and leave at right angles. Never step in the trail itself, but step over it with a giant step. You will be filling in your tracks in the end, but the less human sign the better. Some of my trapper friends try to hollow out a spot from the side, directly under a paw print in the snow and set their trap pan directly under the print. What I have found is that most of the time the trail is packed down from use and from warm days and cold nights and has become frozen and hard. I will address this problem and the solution in the following instructions.

The first thing to address is the trap to use for this set. I recommend a No.3 double coil, but a No.2 four coil will work as well. Attached to the trap, I use a long (six-foot) clean, dyed, and waxed chain with at least three swivels and a grapple at the end. If you do not have a chain and grapple, you can use a cable attached to the end of your trap chain, tied off to a drag or sapling, but the chain and grapple will work the best. More times than not, I will use two traps, set ten inches apart from center of pan

to center of pan. I do not use a pan cover for this set; rather, I block the pan with a purchased pan blocker, piece of cleaned, odorless wool, or fluffy polyester filling from a new modern non-down pillow. You will need a container of sorts, a small clean bucket, some waxed dirt or several pieces of waxed paper cut to a size that is one inch larger all around than your set trap, and a long handle *clean* broom. Approach the trail at right angles, as stated before. Pick a spot on the trail that is relatively straight for at least twenty feet. Have your trap or traps set before you approach the trail. Now that you have the exact place picked out where you intend to set your traps, and standing on one side of the trail, remove a six- to eight-inch-wide and two-foot-long section of the snow from the trail. Put this snow in your bucket. Remove any sticks that may protrude; dead leaves are okay to leave. Scrape this two-foot-long section until it is relatively level. If you have waxed dirt, place enough waxed dirt where you intend to place your traps about an inch in depth, and lightly tamp with the back side of your clean gloved hand. If you are not using waxed dirt, place three to four layers of waxed paper down. Now press your trap into the waxed dirt, positioned so that the coyote will step between the jaws rather than over the jaws, and firm the dirt up around the trap jaws. Lead the trap chain away from the trail at right angles for at least two feet or more and cover any remaining chain with some snow. Next sift enough waxed dirt over the trap to just cover the jaws and springs, leaving the pan exposed. Using your sifter, sift the snow you removed and saved over your traps, enough snow to completely cover your trap with at least one to two inches. If you need more snow, use more, taken from at least three feet away. Make sure the two-foot-long area you set your trap is at the same elevation of the rest of the trail. Use more snow to accomplish this if necessary. Now I usually sift additional snow over the trail at least four feet in both directions from my traps, up and down the trail. You can make simulated tracks with the end of the broom handle in this newly sifted snow, and very carefully right over your traps as well. Fill in your tracks with snow and

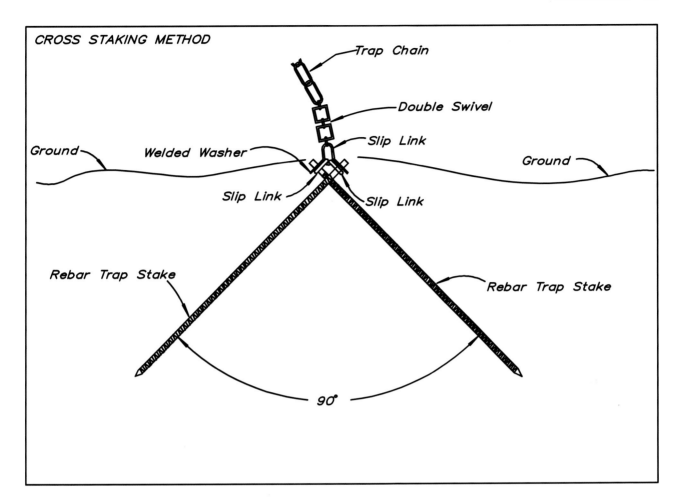

blending the filled-in tracks with your broom as you back away from the set, the way you came in, for about eight feet. When checking your sets, approach no closer than necessary. After a catch, it is much easier.

Special Note: When setting a coyote set in very sandy or lose ground, where you suspect that one stake may not hold the catch, you can use two stakes. This is customarily called "Cross Staking." What you do is drive two, usually a little longer iron stakes, each equipped with a slip link, into the ground at about a 45-degree angle to the ground, in opposite directions, which puts them at about ninety degrees to each other. The top of the stakes should be touching each other so you are able to put a third slip link connecting the two slip links on the stakes. To the third slip link attach a swivel; the other end of the swivel should be attached to the end of your trap chain. This cross staking should hold the biggest coyotes in the worst soil conditions.

Waxed Dirt Recipe

When land trapping with dirt sets, whether they are flat set sets, dirt hole sets, mound sets, blind sets, or even cubbies, and you are experiencing wet conditions such as snow, freezing and thawing, or just plain constant freezing conditions, the best way to have an effective functioning set is the use of waxed dirt. There are many antifreeze powders and salt mixtures which can rust your traps that are available on the market. I have tried most of them, with limited success. In my opinion the best, most effective and productive way I know of is the use of waxed dirt.

I wish I had known about this stuff years ago, as it would have saved me an enormous amount of hard work and heartache. To check your set, see that the animal has worked your set, taken the bait, and your trap is still there frozen in place and unfired is disappointing, to say the least. One of the features of antifreeze powders and salt-based mixtures that I highly dislike is how it leaves you with a well-defined wet spot over and around your concealed trap. Waxed dirt does not melt snow or frozen ground, it just gives you a waterproof material which will not freeze. When prepared properly it does not absorb any moisture and will still allow your trap to function properly in sub-freezing conditions. If it snows after you set your trap, the set is perfectly concealed, with no melted areas; using antifreezes or salt makes it look completely unnatural.

You should make your own batch of waxed dirt in advance and store it for future use as weather conditions deteriorate. It can be made anytime of the year, but it is much more work and takes a lot longer to produce in colder seasons. I strongly advise making it in the summer. There are several ways to produce waxed dirt; some just use the heat of the sun, others use a torch and a cement mixer for larger batches. The following is the method that I personally have used and had the best success with.

In the following instructions, you can either use sifted dirt from a local clean source, or purchase washed masonry sand from a gravel bank. I prefer to use washed masonry sand for a few reasons. First, if you use dirt that you simply dug from a local spot, it must be well sifted, free of organic material like sticks, twigs, and leaves, and dried. This material can be utilized, but it is more time consuming and messy. I am usually short of time, so I personally opt for clean masonry sand. Secondly, it is of one uniform size and dries much more quickly.

You will need a large, flat, odorless surface like sheet of plywood or sheet of stiff plastic, which can be purchased at most home improvement stores. Plastic is better in my opinion, because it does not absorb foreign odors and can be washed and left out in the sun to dry without any damage to it. You'll also need a few large flat pans (roasting pans), a pair of clean thick gloves, a container in which to store your finished product (a large trash can or five-gallon bucket, both with tops), non-scented, flaked wax, and an odorless, controllable heat source. For a heat source I use my cleaned gas grill. I usually prepare a batch consisting of a five-gallon bucket.

The first step, if preparing your mixture outdoors, is to pick a sunny, hot day, spread out a five-gallon bucket full of sand or well-sifted dirt onto your flat surface, about a half an inch in depth. To speed things up I put down a heavy sheet of black plastic or black tarp to spread the dirt out on. Leave it in the sun to dry, removing all of the moisture, working it around several times an hour; I use the flat of an unused, large paint-mixing stick to move it around, to expose it all to the air and sun. A trowel will work just as well.

When completely dry, it should be of a dusty, powdery consistency. Making sure that the dirt or sand is bone dry is the most important factor in producing an ideal finished product. When you have dried the sand or dirt and it is still widely spread out on your flat surface, wearing gloves, sprinkle about two and a half pounds of flaked wax evenly on the top of the dirt, making sure it is distributed equally throughout the dirt. Don't worry about using too much wax; you can't overdo things easily. Next, mix the wax well into the bone-dry dirt or sand. Collect the dirt and wax mixture into a clean bucket. Now, in a roasting pan or other large metal container (I use a large turkey roasting pan) fill the container half full with the wax/dirt mixture. I place the pan on my gas grill set on the lowest possible setting. You only need to heat the entire dirt mixture to about 150°F. When the mixture on the edges of the pan start to appear wet, I start to constantly mix the wax-impregnated dirt until it all appears wet. At that point I remove the pan from the heat and empty the entire container onto my flat surface, minus the black tarp, to cool. Spread the waxed dirt out as much as possible so it will cool quickly. Constantly move the mixture around until it is cooled to room temperature. If there are any small clumps, I put them through my sifter. If done correctly there should not be any clumps at all. Once *completely* cooled, you can now pour it into your storage container and cover. Repeat the process until you have waxed all of the dirt in the five-gallon bucket. Some trappers like to store their waxed dirt in large containers, but I prefer to store it in covered five-gallon buckets. These are much lighter to handle and move around, they are stackable, and you can see at a glance just how much dirt you have on hand.. This also cuts down on the chances of foreign orders contaminating the entire batch. It is not easy or cheap to produce, but worth every penny and minute of your time, if you intend to do any land trapping in freezing conditions.

The Raccoon, *Procyon Lotor,* "Mr. Ring Tail"

Raccoons are native to North America and can be found across the continent, from Panama to Canada, East Coast to West Coast and everywhere in between. They are, in my opinion, the most important fur-bearer, in terms of revenue. Their fur has been used for centuries—for hats, coats, trade, and even as

money. Some Indian tribes held them in such high regard that they would not hunt or trap them.

Raccoons vary greatly in both size and color. Average adults range in size from between fifteen to thirty pounds full grown in the wild, depending on the geographic location. Generally speaking, raccoons will be smaller at the lower latitudes and larger at the higher latitudes. They will measure about sixteen to thirty inches in length, head to base of tail, about ten inches high at the shoulder, and have a ringed tail of about twelve inches long, erect ears, and the well-known facial mask.

Raccoons come in a variety of color phases; I have seen them from almost very light to very dark, nearly melanistic. But most are a grayish black, due to their thick dense underfur and long guard hairs.

The nimble raccoon, with agile forepaws. (Photo Credit: Getty Images.)

Raccoon scat, filled with wild grape skins and seeds.

When they are healthy and prime they look silverish due the guard hairs. I have run hounds for raccoons most of my life and have seen a wide and varying lot of color, from blonde ones to pure black ones.

I also have had them for pets and have known a lot of fellow hunters and trappers who have also had them for pets. I was good friends with a gentleman named Les Perlee, who had one that was sixty pounds and loved marshmallows and circus peanuts. In the wild they live on average three to four years, but as pets they can live twenty-plus years. Here in the Northeast they breed from January to March. Males do not have any part in raising the kits. In fact, the females have to protect the kits or cubs from the males, as the males are apt to kill the kits. Gestation period is about sixty-five days, giving birth to between two to five kits or cubs. I have personally seen as many as nine, but that is the exception, not the rule. Kits or cubs stay with the mother until fall, when they are more than able to take care of themselves.

At dispersal time the males usually range out much more than the females. Females tend to stay in the same territory that their mother covered, but males have been known to range out as much as fifteen miles. The kits are born blind and deaf but still have the famous face mask evident, but it's not as pronounced. Raccoons are mostly nocturnal but in the fall I have observed them out at all hours, sleeping in trees next to large food sources, feeding and sleeping and feeding again, as they are building themselves up for winter. They have very dexterous front paws and use them to accomplish amazing tasks. They have a great sense of touch. Their feet are not webbed, but they love water and are great swimmers and have been known to drown coon dogs when fighting in deep water. They have a great sense of smell and even better hearing. Raccoons have poor long distance sight, but can see exceptionally well at dusk and full darkness. Their hearing is exceptional, such that they can hear an earthworm moving in shallow earth.

Raccoons will eat almost everything: insects, bee hives with honey, birds (too often my chickens), fish,

A female raccoon outside of her den tree.

fruits, berries, vegetables, corn (they especially love corn in milk stage, be it sweet or cattle corn), crawfish, mussels, frogs, bird's eggs, snakes, mice, rats, baby rabbits in the nest, acorns, wild grapes (a favorite), and we all know what they can do to a garbage can.

In my opinion, raccoons make good pets for a person experienced in handling wild animals. President Calvin Coolidge kept a pet raccoon during his term in the White House. The age at which you obtain a raccoon for a pet is very important, for the younger they are, the easier they are to tame and stay tame. The best age in my opinion is just after they are able to live without their mother's milk and able to eat solid food. They will, however, become aggressive during breeding season.

I had a pet raccoon named Bandit, yet I probably should have named him Houdini. At a very young age, he was able to unlatch his cage—which was on an enclosed porch—open the door to the inside of the house, find his way upstairs into our bedroom, and climb up onto the bed to sleep above my pillow. This, as you might have suspected, did not go over very well with my wife. I kept finding new ways to fasten the door of his cage, but in time he would figure out how to open it. I finally resorted to using a small padlock. To sum it up, raccoons are highly intelligent and can use their front paws to perform amazing tasks. The reason I am telling you all this is that you can use the fact that they will rely on their front paws—almost like we use our hands—to obtain an advantage when trapping.

Raccoons are like gold, they are where you find them, from cities to wilderness, from low-lying swamps to mountain tops. They inhabit barns, sheds, open silos, houses (both empty and inhabited ones), hollow trees (called den trees), caves, woodchuck holes, large drainage pipes, junked cars, dilapidated buildings, or any other place that is out of the weather and where they feel safe. There are potential problems when trapping raccoons that you should always keep in mind, primarily because they live among humans and their pets. I strongly advise, and will mention it again, that you have to use a different kind of trap and bait when trapping raccoons anywhere near residential areas.

Raccoons tend to travel the same areas that their mother took them in spring and summer during trapping season.

They travel along stream banks, through swamps, as well as ridges. Scouting these places in late summer will pay off greatly in the fall trapping season. As I previously mentioned, they live in hollow trees called den trees. I strongly suggest that you NEVER place a leg hold set within one hundred fifty feet of a den tree, especially if it is a blind set by the den tree or it is baited with meat or fish. There a two main reasons for this. The first is that a raccoon being hunted—with coon hounds that are hot on their trail—will most often try to make it back to the safety of its den tree. If you make your set close to that den tree, you will inevitably catch the coon dog in the trap and not the raccoon. This will most likely result in a missing trap and a very angry coon hunter, which may result in confrontation, if not retaliation. I have personally witnessed both, having hunted raccoons with hounds since the age of thirteen. In addition, you may be asked or ordered not to trap on that property at all, which may contain other furbearers, by the owner of the property. The second reason raccoons are just like all furbearers; though they are a renewable resource, never try to take all of them, always leave some to live on and repopulate. It is the prudent and ethical thing to do!

The classic "bank robber" mask of the raccoon. (Photo Credit: Getty Images.)

When trapping raccoons close to inhabited houses or barns, it is wise and ethical to use a live trap the style Havahart markets. There are several brands to choose from; all work on the same principal, and are very effective. I guarantee that family pets—mostly dogs and cats—will be attracted to those sets that are made for raccoons. These are people's family pets and pets will wander away from their backyards. It does not do you any service, to yourself or the sport, to injure or even kill someone's pet that they love and adore. All you will accomplish is angering them beyond belief and give yourself a bad reputation, as well as the sport of trapping in general. The fastest way I can think of to be banned from trapping a piece of property is to catch, injure, or kill someone's pet, whether the landowner's or his neighbor's. I will tell you how to most effectively deploy a live trap later on in this chapter.

Honestly, it is very difficult to release a scared and injured cat or dog from a leghold trap without becoming injured yourself, especially when you are by yourself. Sometimes an animal—especially a large dog—will attack when released. I have had it happen to me more than once. If you insist on setting a leghold trap in an area that might have pets running around, I strongly recommend the use of a "soft catch" style of leghold trap, and that you check your traps more than once per day. This will minimize the pet's injury and shorten the time that pet was in the trap.

Baits

Baits for raccoons vary from honey to vegetable to meat, depending on the set and set location. With each different set I will teach you about, I will give you different baits to choose from, and for very important reasons. While I am briefly talking about baits, *never*—I repeat, *never*—use commercial cat food or dog food as bait (canned or dry) for a leghold set in populated areas. Some water sets are exempt from this rule. There are so many more effective baits that can be utilized, so there is no point in using pet food at all. It may be tempting, but highly unwise.

Depending on set location, and whether you use a land set or water set, the most effective baits can differ. Example: you would not want to use a parched corn and honey mixture, or marshmallows, for bait at a stream set, but would likely use a fish- or meat-based bait that would also be an attractant to, say, a passing mink, muskrat, or otter.

Here is one recipe for great homemade bait (raccoon bait balls), which can be prepared relatively inexpensively and will work in all weather conditions, giving off a very alluring scent:

2 cans of sardines, the cheaper the better
2 to 3 tablespoons of bacon drippings
2 to 3 tablespoons of vegetable oil
1 package of fruit pectin
1 tablespoon of anise oil
Corn starch or flour

Wearing surgical or rubber gloves, empty the entire contents of the two cans of sardines into a large mixing bowl. With a large fork, crush up the sardines. Add to these one to two tablespoons of bacon drippings. Mix thoroughly. Then add in your vegetable oil and again mix thoroughly. Add in one package of fruit pectin, again mixing thoroughly. Then add one tablespoon of anise oil. Mix this in well. You now should have a gooey mixture that needs to be thickened. Add corn starch a little at a time, working it into the mixture thoroughly, until you have a consistency of cookie dough. Now make ping-pong-ball-sized balls, store them in a freezer bag, and freeze them for use when you need them. Some people put them in ice cube trays and then freeze them until ready for use. If you choose to use ice cube trays, put the trays in large freezer bags and seal before freezing. You can bring the cubes or balls on your trap line frozen, as they will thaw out on site in a little while, giving off a tempting scent which any self-respecting raccoon cannot pass up. These bait balls are great for cubby sets, hollow tree, and log sets.

Sets

The Cubby

In my opinion, this is the most productive set for raccoon among the land sets, because if constructed properly it can be used year after year, can be set up fairly quickly, and can be pre-baited. They can range from simple stick or log construction, to plastic or metal buckets, to four-inch-diameter or larger PVC pipe, to rock or stone construction. The bait/lure at a cubby set will last a lot longer because it is generally out of the weather.

The basic principle with this set is very simple. You have a baited enclosure, the cubby, and a trap set at the entrance. When dry land trapping with cubbies, I never set up a cubby right on a raccoon trail, but always a few feet to a few yards off the trail. This keeps from getting non-target catches to a minimum. You will always get them, but not as many.

I prefer stone construction, especially if you know that you will be able to trap the same territory year after year and if the flat stones are readily available on site or able to be built right into existing stonewalls. Here in upstate New York, there are many stone walls along open fields, streams, and through wooded areas that were open fields hundreds of years ago. Raccoons love to walk on stone walls while looking for food and will defecate on these walls; hence it is a win-win placement for a cubby. Also, the stone cubbies blend right in and are not easily spotted, keeping the losses of both traps and furbearers to thieves at a minimum. I construct a stone box-shaped cubby, inside dimension of about one foot square, and eight inches to a foot high, with a heavy stone secured top, and with *only one* opening giving access to the bait, right against the tight base of the stone wall. If a stone wall is not available to build against, you can use a large

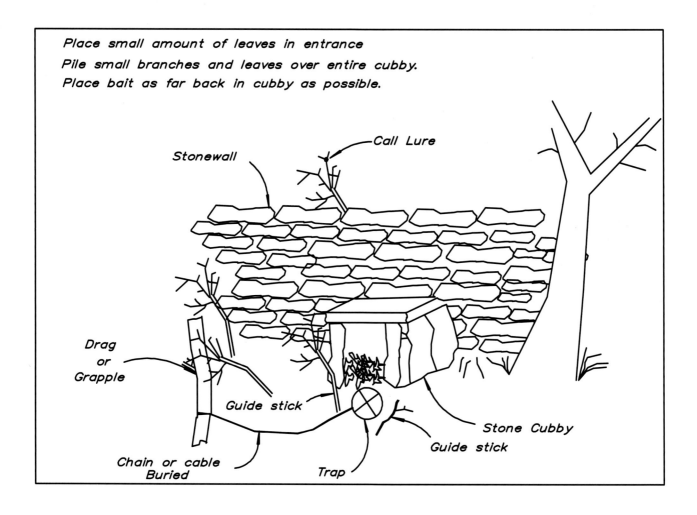

Place small amount of leaves in entrance
Pile small branches and leaves over entire cubby.
Place bait as far back in cubby as possible.

Stonewall
Call Lure
Drag or Grapple
Guide stick
Stone Cubby
Guide stick
Chain or cable Buried
Trap

A natural cubby is an obvious place to make a cubby set for raccoon.

tree, large log, steep bank, or boulder. I usually cover the cubby with small branches and leaves. The opening can be rectangular or triangular in shape, makes no difference. I make the opening about six inches wide, but no larger than eight inches, and about the same height. I solidly bed a clean, odor-free #1½ or # 2, double-coil spring trap, keeping the closest jaw no closer than about three inches from the edge of the entrance and about one to two inches off center. The reason to solidly bed a clean, odorless trap is that this set will also take an occasional gray fox.

You can stake the trap right there, but I find a large drag or long-chained grapple will work much better as it stops the trapped animal from tearing apart the cubby that you worked hard to properly construct. Cover the trap with some sifted dirt, blend it in, and use a trap pan cover. I use cleaned plastic screen cut to size, boiled and dyed canvas, or crinkled wax paper as a pan cover. If using a drag or grapple, dig or push the chain or cable into the ground about an inch, for about at least eighteen to twenty-four inches away from the trap. The reason for this is that if you leave it on the surface and just cover it with leaves, the animal may trip or get tangled on it and dislodge the well-bedded trap, leaving you with a sprung trap, no bait, and no raccoon. Place your bait of choice (preferably meat- or fish-based), and/ or lure on a small, thin flat rock, placed as far back in the cubby as possible. Clean up the site as much as you can, leaving it as close to how you found it as possible. As stated before, the cubby can be made up from a number of various materials. You can use on-site materials such as logs, sticks, base of hollow trees, natural rock formations, and so on. Some trappers like to build them at home out of dimensional lumber and bring them to their trap line. No matter

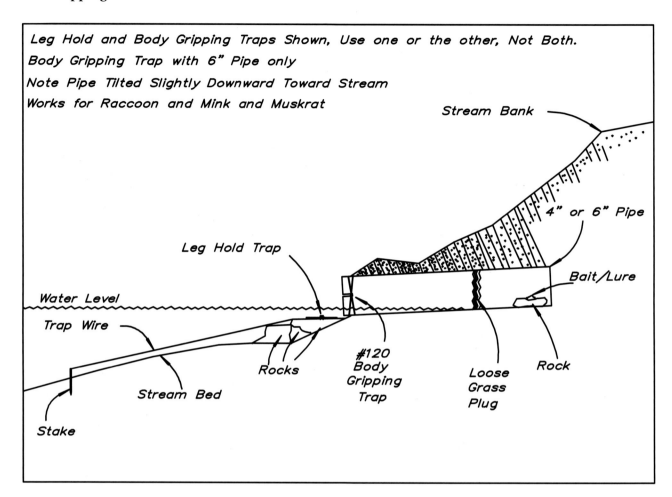

Leg Hold and Body Gripping Traps Shown, Use one or the other, Not Both.
Body Gripping Trap with 6" Pipe only
Note Pipe Tilted Slightly Downward Toward Stream
Works for Raccoon and Mink and Muskrat

which type you decide to utilize, the principle is the same.

You might be wondering why I do not use a body-gripping trap for this set, as in theory it would work perfectly. Well, unless you are wilderness trapping, you run the risk of an occasional cat or dog visiting your cubby set. Body-gripping traps are designed to kill instantly, so I don't use them on dry-land cubby sets. Why kill something for no reason? You can always let some cat or dog, which is someone's adored pet, out of a leghold trap alive. In some states it is illegal to set raccoon-size body-gripping traps lower than a specified distance up off the ground unless they are water sets. This makes perfect sense to me.

The PVC Pipe Set

Along streams, the PVC pipe set is much more advantageous than just a pocket in the bank. Although, pockets—be they natural or dug-out—are very effective, I like the four-inch and six-inch-diameter pipes, about twelve to eighteen inches long. You can just dig the pipe right into the bank, or if no suitable bank exists, set it where it needs to be and cover it with dirt, rocks, mud, and debris. You can pick the elevation and pitch of the cubby that is most advantageous to that particular site location. Mink and muskrats also like to investigate these holes. Most of the time, one end will be plugged. As a general rule, I like to set the cubby/pipe an inch or two above the water elevation, and place the trap just under the water at the front end of the pipe.

The Double Catch

There are a few rare occasions where there is a very high raccoon population; for that I will use a three- to four-foot-long, six-inch-diameter PVC pipe, open on both ends. I simply place the pipe on the ground—whether muddy, wet, or dry. I will drive a few short stakes on both sides of the pipe to hold it in place, cover this pipe with large stones and mud, burying all but the very ends. My trap size of choice for this set

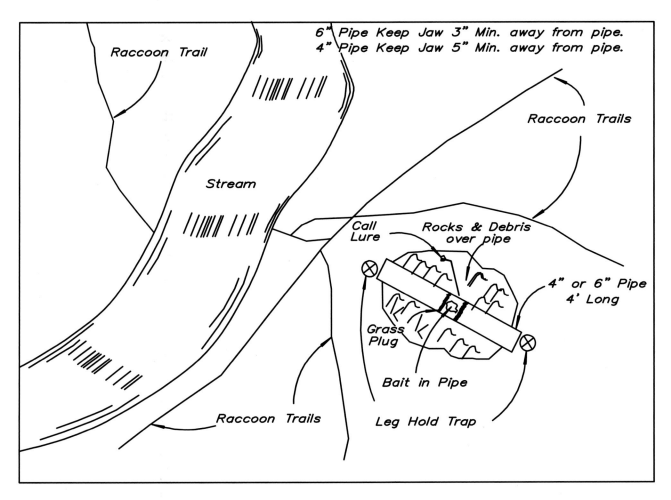

The raccoon is inquisitive, as well as dexterous. (Photo Credit: Getty Images.)

is the #1½ double-coil spring, though double long-spring traps work equally well. Place and bed a trap at each end of the pipe, so that the closest jaw is at least three inches away from the end of the pipe. Conceal the traps as best as you can, under water if possible. You can stake them fast, but I prefer a large drag or long-chained grapple. Not only does this allow the trapped animal to move away from the set, keeping it ready for the next raccoon, but it helps to keep the set hidden from hunters or thieves.

Place your bait/lure up in the middle of the pipe. Place some leaves or a grass plug on each side of the bait. Place a bit of raccoon call lure on a twig or stick protruding up from the area at the middle of the pipe. Multiple catches are possible in one night from the one set.

In water sets for raccoons, the body-gripping style traps are a very efficient choice, which may be utilized with minimal chance of catching a cat or dog, if set correctly. The body-gripping trap that you see today was perfected by Frank Conibear in Canada in the 1950s. I have caught numerous amounts of raccoons with just a #120 Conibear and a piece of six-inch-diameter PVC pipe. This set also works well on muskrats and mink. Take a twelve- to eighteen-inch length of six-inch-diameter PVC pipe and at one end cut a slot wide enough to freely accept the springs of the set trap, about four inches long. I usually place the pipe so that about one to two inches of water fills the front part of the pipe, no more, and set it right on the bank of a stream or swamp, where there is sign of raccoons walking along the bank. I place a stone in the back of the pipe to set my bait/lure on, to keep it up and out of the water that may be in the pipe. If the pipe is not dug into a bank, make sure the non-trap end is totally plugged, so all odors from your bait only come out the trap end of the pipe. I usually set the trigger wires in an upside down "L" configuration. Anchor the trap to a root, or drag, or stake. Anchor it well so no other animal can walk off with your prize. Camouflage the set with grass from the set site. Remember to undo the spring hooks on both sides; while this sounds obvious, I have walked away—more than once—with the spring hooks attached and came back next morning to find bait gone and trap lying outside the cubby, un-sprung.

The biggest body-gripping trap I personally use for raccoon is the #160, having a six-inch by six-inch jaw opening. I use them with hand-dug pocket sets at the waterline, only because you need an eight-inch-diameter pipe to utilize this trap. If you want to use eight-inch pipes and are willing to carry them

A 1½ double long spring, perfect for raccoon.

around your trap line, they work very well. The #120 works well for me and I believe if it is not broken, don't fix it!

If you choose not to go the body-gripping trap route, and choose to use a leghold trap instead, use #1½ or #1.75 coil-spring trap; long spring traps work just as well but are a little more difficult to conceal. Place your trap so that the closest jaw is no closer than three inches away from the edge of the pipe. If possible, bed traps about one to two inches below the water; you can use a flat rock under the trap if the water is too deep. Anchor this trap securely to a drag, as staking may come loose in the muddy conditions.

Another set to look for when using leghold traps is a large tree on the stream bank, very close to the water, which has a hollow spot or exposed roots overhanging on the stream side, creating a natural pocket. Set your trap in the water, again one to two inches below the water, and bait the hollow pocket. Use a gland lure just above the opening. This is a good set for mink as well.

The Shining Set

This set was handed down to me when I was a young teenager, in the 1960s, by Harold Holsapple of Linlithgo, New York. He was a northern longline trapper, yet also trapped locally. This set is premised on the fact that raccoons are attracted to shiny objects. Look for a spot along a stream, which has clear water running during normal conditions. Take some aluminum foil, and wrap the pan of the trap completely with the foil, shiny side up. Set the trap about six inches out into the water so it is visible from the shore. Seat the trap in about two inches of water and conceal it with sand or mud, all but the shiny pan. Anchor the trap to a large drag or rock. When Mr. Holsapple first told me about this set I have to admit I was skeptical; it sounded too easy, but I took two raccoons that fall with this set. He also told me that you can wire a live, declawed crayfish to the pan, setting the trap close to the shore. I have never tried it, but it makes sense that it would work. I would use a #2 double coil or long spring for this set.

Cage Trap or Live Trap Sets

In areas close to houses and barns, where house pets are always around, I strongly recommend that you use only a cage trap, the style Havahart markets. These traps can be placed anywhere, without fear of injuring any non-targeted animals. I recommend only purchasing the style that opens up at both ends (double door). For raccoons the best size to use measures approximately 12½ by 14½ by 36 inches. Most wild animals will enter a cage trap more willingly if they can see right through them. Additionally, if you want to set the trap directly on and in line with a heavily used trail, they will likely go right through without any hesitation, rather than view the trap as an obstruction in their regularly traveled trail. Another advantage with this style trap is that you can use a wide spectrum of baits, from common table scraps to sophisticated commercial trapping bait. You can pre-bait the area, getting the raccoons used to enjoying your bait, so when you place your baited cage trap, they will show little hesitation to enter. Always anchor or steady your cage traps well, stopping them from premature closing if the raccoon climbs on top of it. I use a large rock or any other weighted object that is at hand, or just plain wire it down to a stake or stakes.

When placing a cage trap, if it is not inside a building I customarily camouflage it with branches and leaves so that it looks like a tunnel, which raccoons encounter numerous times every day, greatly reducing any hesitation to enter the trap. When trapping close or actually inside buildings you can use marshmallows, cooked, fatty meats, bacon, sardines, or honey-flavored bread as bait; this list goes on and on. When trapping inside or right outside of a building, I usually place the trap up against the building. Raccoons naturally travel along the walls of buildings, making a successful catch sooner than later. When you become proficient with these traps, extra money can be made removing nuisance raccoons from residential areas and buildings. People are willing to pay good money to have raccoons removed humanely, unharmed, with no danger to their pets, and depending on the time of year, you even get to keep the money from the fur as well. Note: if you are releasing the trapped nuisance raccoons, take them at least ten miles away from the site before releasing them, otherwise you might end up catching the same raccoons over and over again.

When utilizing the cage trap out in the wild, I usually chain them down with a length of dog chain, wrap the non-trap end around a substantial tree or other large stationary object, and padlock the chain. People will steal these traps more often than leghold traps, for the simple reason that they are much more visible and harder to conceal. Unlike leghold traps, cage traps take only minutes to reset, the trapped raccoon is usually very clean, and non-target animals can be released without injury to the animal and, more importantly, injury to you.

Dog-Proof Coon Sets

There are two ways to make an (almost) dog-proof

raccoon set; as nothing is 100 percent that I know of. One is to buy a dog-proof coon trap, and the other is to utilize your size #1½, #1¾ and #2 leg hold traps, long spring or coil spring. I will give you detailed instructions on how to make a "dog proof "set utilizing leg hold traps a little later.

If you plan to use the commercially manufactured dog-proof coon trap, there are a few things you should know before you go out and buy a bunch of them. These manufactured traps come in many styles, but all function about the same way. The principle workings of the trap exploits the dexterity of the raccoon's front paws. The trap operates on the premise that the raccoon will reach into the cylinder to extract the food or bait, thus setting off the trap. They are compact and relatively light. Most have a spike or spade to support the trap plus a #2 machine chain attached with two to three swivels. Some have an exposed dog and some just have a latch.

A dog-proof coon trap allows the trapper to avoid unwanted catches of household pets.

The traps are about eight inches long overall, with an approximate four-inch cylinder being part of it. The bait cylinder openings are between one and one-quarter and one and one-half inches in diameter. Most have a round cylinder, though some are rectangular. All that I have seen have a heavy wire-type bail or snare that holds the raccoon's foot. Some are made in the USA and some are not; I always try to buy things made in the USA, as they seem to be made better; plus you are keeping a fellow American in a job. Traps run from about $12 to $16, and are cheaper when you buy a half-dozen or more at a time. The only major difference I want to stress is in the firing mechanisms. Some fire *only* when the bait/trigger is pulled on, with upward pressure by the raccoon's front foot. The other type fires when upward or downward pressure is applied. Your chances are obviously better for a catch with the one that fires in both directions, but there are some subtle drawbacks to this. One is that if you fill the bait cylinder to the top, it can be set off by animals other than raccoons, like squirrels, chipmunks, and the like. Other non-target animals may be dogs and cats, which defeats the whole purpose for using these style traps.

If the bait cylinder if filled to the top with food/bait and the dog licks the bait, it will inevitability catch him by the tongue. As for cats, they have a habit of pawing at things, and if the cat pushes down on the bait in the cylinder you have just caught a cat! Because of this I *never* fill a push/pull type of trap up to the very top with bait, only to about one inch shy of the top. When using the pull-only kind, you can fill right to the top.

This information comes in handy when placing these traps in or near buildings with pets nearby. Another thing to remember is to never use fish oil or other baits that would attract a dog to lick it on or inside the cylinder of the push-pull type. Rather put in a corn- or grain-type bait, and put your fish oil or other attractor outside, right next to the trap. When placing these traps on a coon trail, I put them right smack in the middle of the trail, so the raccoon has to go around it to avoid it; odds are he won't. When placing them off a trail, even a very short distance, inches, and especially when the trail is going up a steep bank, I tilt the trap 45 degrees so the raccoon has an easy view of what's inside the cylinder. Always set it so the dog or latch is upward. These traps work well where a dirt set is not practical because of muddy or freezing soil conditions. Some traps come in colors or people paint them white. I have talked to other trappers who have done this and they say that amount of non-target animals caught will go up. My advice is to leave them alone and do not paint them.

Another great place for these style traps is on stone walls. I have noticed that raccoons along with other furbearers like to run along the tops of stone walls. You can see spots where they have deposited their scat in piles, obviously spending a lot of time in that location, multiple times. Locations where wild grapes are abundant or growing on trees right next to the walls are a great spot to look. You can just remove a few stones, set your trap, and replace the stones, making it look like you were never even there. It is a good idea to mark the spot a few feet away so you can find your own trap without any difficulty when the time comes.

Dog-Proof Leghold Sets (one of my favorites)

This kind of "dog-proof trap set" is constructed in the following manner: Cut an eighteen-inch by eighteen-inch square (or larger) piece of plywood or paneling, one-quarter to three-eighths inches thick; I prefer the three-eighth-inch thickness for durability. Exactly in the center, drill a one and one-half-inch-diameter hole through it; I like to take a rasp and smooth the edges a bit. Now, at the set site, dig a hole wide enough to bed your trap and chain to a depth of five inches, no less. The chain should be at least three feet long. Drive your trap stake in one corner of the hole. Set the dirt from the hole at least two feet away from hole. Level the ground around the hole at least one foot in all directions. Stake and bed your trap well, set it to a hair trigger, in the hole

Raccoon tracks—this is the front paw—are similar to human handprints.

with the chain set off to one side. Bed it well so there is no movement. Now place your bait—I use corn scented with honey or parched corn, with honey rolled into marble-size balls or a raccoon bait ball on the pan. Place a few pieces around the pan as well. Next take your piece of plywood and set it on the leveled ground directly over the pan of the trap in the hole.

Press down on the board in various spots to see that it does not move when pressure is applied. If it does, take down any high spots and reset plywood. Now take the dirt from digging the trap hole and cover the edges of the plywood, blending it in with the surrounding ground toughly. If additional dirt is needed, use soil available nearby. Now place some bait pieces, corn, or other attractant (some trappers even use dry dog or cat food) around the

hole on the top of the plywood. The raccoon will eat up the pieces on the ground and, wanting more, will put its front paw into the hole and fire the trap. This set is also very safe from your trap being damaged by someone running it over with a quad or ATV or even a tractor, as they will just go over it unnoticed. Never use sheet metal instead of wood, because it will severely cut up the trapped animal's foot and cause much unnecessary pain and suffering to the trapped animal (this is the reason I use a wood rasp to smooth the edges of the top of the hole). This set will also work well in freezing and thawing conditions.

This set works great along edges of corn fields, and where raccoon damage is evident. They do most of their destruction when the corn is milky but they return to these spots well into trapping season.

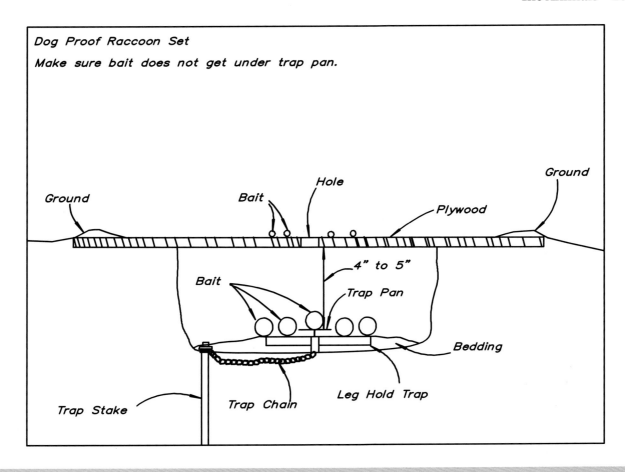

Dog Proof Raccoon Set
Make sure bait does not get under trap pan.

Ground · Bait · Hole · Ground · Plywood · 4" to 5" · Trap Pan · Bait · Bedding · Leg Hold Trap · Trap Stake · Trap Chain

Parched Corn and Honey Balls Recipe

The way I make parched corn is as follows: I obtain sweet corn when ripe. I let this corn, right on the cob, dry in a well-ventilated place for about six weeks or until dry. You can tell when it is dry and ready by attempting to twist the kernels off the cob in the palm of your hand. If it is ready, they will twist right off. De-cob all the corn that is ready. Now take a pan; I use a cast-iron pan as I feel this works best. Grease the entire pan with vegetable oil or lard. Preheat the pan on a low heat. When warm, fill the bottom of the pan with enough corn to fill the entire bottom about a half inch in depth. Stir the corn as it cooks until it is golden brown in color; some kernels my even pop. Remove that batch and place the parched corn on a flat surface; spread it out and let it completely cool. Repeat the process until all your corn is parched. Now grind it into a powder, using a blender, a coffee grinder, or a simple mortar and pestle. Sift the powder and regrind pieces that do not pass through your sifter. Next I place the parched corn powder in a bowl and work in some honey, a little at a time, until it becomes the consistency of dry cookie dough. Then roll the mixture into marble-size balls or roll it into long round pieces and just cut off pieces with a sharp knife. Place them on a cookie sheet lined with wax paper. Let them stand for several hours. (Tip: Place your jar of honey in hot water, deep enough so that most of the honey inside the jar is surrounded by hot water for about twenty minutes. This makes the honey become more lique-fied and much easier to work in to the parched corn.) These balls are actually edible, but they are meant for Mr. Ring Tail. I have eaten them myself when on my trap line. Store any unused parched corn or parched corn powder in a muslin bag, in a well-ventilated place, and it will last for months. Parched corn has been carried by trappers, frontiersmen, explorers, and cowboys for centuries because it is very nutritious, very light, and would last for months when they were away from civilization.

Log Crossing and Log Sets

A log crossing a stream—acting like a bridge—is always a good place for a raccoon set. Most trapping books advocate notching out a depression in the log and setting a trap; it is usually a blind set with a stepping stick. This will work but, in my opinion, it will catch more non-target animals than the ones you intend to trap; you will catch more squirrels than raccoons. I agree the log crossing the stream will funnel furbearers at that location. You can still use this condition to your advantage, but instead of the blind set on the log I make either a dirt set or pocket set at each end of the log if the situation permits. It is more productive, takes much less time to prepare, and much less non-target catches. A lot of times you'll come across a spot where a tree or log has fallen into the stream, pond or deep swamp, rendering the log partially submerged. Raccoons frequently visit these spots as well. At these sets I notch out a spot two inches below the water. Secure the trap in the notch with heavy mud. Right opposite the trap against the log I place a thin stick in the mud so it sticks out of the water about 18 to 24 inches above the trap. On this stick I place a cotton ball or piece of clean wool attached to the stick with a twist tie, and on that I place a good raccoon food lure or raccoon call lure. Secure the trap to the log lower than the set with wire or a large fence staple. This set will take mink as well as raccoons.

Another spot that naturally involves logs is where a hollow log or half of a hollow log has lodged itself up against the bank of the stream with water flowing through it. I usually place a trap at the downstream end of the hollow log under the water so the trap in about 1 to 2 inches under the water. If the water is too deep you can use a flat rock to bring the trap up to the desirable level. Place trap so the jaw is about two to three inches away from the end of the log. Place a good gland lure on the top edge of the downstream end of the log. Secure the trap to a large object, log, rock, or root. This is also a good set for mink.

The Swamp Hillock Set

Swamps and marshlands have hillocks or mounds surrounded by very shallow water or no water at all, just muck. Raccoons will make trails that go between these hillocks rather than over them, making them almost invisible. If you see raccoon sign close to dry land on the edge of the swamp, look for these raccoon trails. These hillocks are a great set, capable of multiple catches. Place your bait on the top of the hillock or mound, using a few pieces of fish, sardines, or raccoon bait balls. Cover the bait well with grass, to keep the birds from eating it. At the base of the hillock place your trap and conceal it with grass. If there are a couple inches of water around the hillocks, that's even better, as it will help to conceal the traps. I usually make these sets in groups of three, picking hillocks at least six feet apart. Secure the traps to a large drag or sapling, as staking is not usually practical in these soil conditions.

Dry Land Dirt Set

The dry land dirt set for raccoons is very similar to the dirt hole set for foxes. The biggest difference is the location, size, bait, and lure used at these sets. For raccoons, location should be very close to trails used by them, as opposed to fox and coyote sets where the foxes and coyotes will follow their noses a long ways to the set. These sets should be in a location that does not flood; the dryer the better. On a dirt hole set for raccoons, I would make the set a few feet or less off their trail. The hole can be almost straight down, with a stone or small log backing on the opposite side of the trap from the bait hole. Dig a trap bed a little larger than the trap you intend to utilize. Bed the trap well so as not to let it move at all and drive your stake right next to the trap or under the trap. I place the trap no closer than three inches from the closest jaw to the edge of the hole, and a little to one side. Use gloves and an odorless trap. Use a pan cover over the pan as described in the chapter on fox sets. Sift dirt over the trap, and blend in with brush or pine bough. Use stepping sticks to guide the raccoon on to the trap pan. Bait with honey and parched corn or raccoon bait balls or muskrat carcass. Place a loose grass plug over the bait. Use a good raccoon gland lure at the top edge of the bait hole. The bait hole should be about six to nine inches deep. If done cleanly, this set will take gray foxes as well.

Bobcat — The Ghost of the Forest

The bobcat is a solitary, beautiful animal.

The North American bobcat—*Lynx rufus*—is a spotted feline that ranges from southern Canada to southern Mexico. It is famous for its short, or bobbed, tail, which ends in black fur, as well as its unique spotted coat. It has small tufts of black hair on its pointed ear tips, and a grayish brown coat. Depending on the region, the bobcat's coat may appear vibrant in color or pale in the more arid environments. Its face has long whiskers and distinctive tufts of hair on its cheeks resembling sideburns. The eyes are yellow in color, with black pupils. A few rare melanistic bobcats have been taken—predominately in Florida—but despite the black coat, the spots are still visible.

The bobcat is equipped with wide, furry paws for silent stalking and razor-sharp nails for a quick kill.

Bobcats resemble the other members of the Lynx species—Canadian lynx, Iberian lynx, and Eurasian lynx—though the bobcat is the smallest of the lot. The hind legs are longer than the front, giving the bobcat a unique gait.

The bobcat is an efficient predator, adaptable to a good number of environments, though it usually prefers solitude in the wild places. They are the prey of other predators—coyotes will wreak havoc on a bobcat population—but can decimate smaller livestock, such as chickens, ducks, and geese. In the wild, the bobcat prefers to prey upon rabbits and hares, insects, small rodents and squirrels, and even deer fawns, though instances of a bobcat taking sheep, goats, and adult deer have been recorded, especially during the lean winter months. When this happens, the bobcat—not unlike his cousin the African leopard—will return several times to feed on the carcass. A bobcat will also scavenge another animal's kill, and some kills have been incorrectly attributed to a bobcat, due to its presence while feeding on the carcass.

Like most felines, the bobcat is a solitary animal, with a wide home range, pairing up only for mating. It is adaptable to a variety of ecosystems, including arboreal forest, semi-desert, swampland, the edges of farmlands and forests, as well as the open prairie of the Great Plains. The bobcat is a brave soul, and will aggressively attack its prey—a characteristic that a trapper can use to his or her advantage. It will mark its territory by making scratching posts, and depositing both urine and feces. A bobcat can range from twenty to fifty inches in length from head to the base of the tail, with the short tail measuring from four to eight inches. They stand between twelve and twenty-four inches high at the shoulder. An adult male cat will weigh between eighteen and forty pounds, with females weighing between ten and thirty pounds. Exceptional specimens have weighed as much as fifty pounds, though that weight/size is a rarity. The larger specimens are located along the northern fringes, usually near the US-Canadian border. Bobcats are crepuscular, meaning they will be most active for a couple of hours before and after sunset and sunrise, as well as throughout the night.

Bobcats pair up to mate during February and March, and the females have an estrous cycle of forty-four days. A litter of two to four kits—sometimes as many as six—is born after a gestation period of sixty to seventy days, with the mother giving birth in a secluded place like a small cave or the security of a hollow log. The young will stay with their mother, who raises them alone, for just about a year, when they are dispersed so the mother may mate again. In the northern climates, kittens may stay with their mothers for as long as eighteen months. One male bobcat may service several females, depending on the population within his home range. The sounds of a courting bobcat can be heard in the deep woods; you'll hear a childlike scream or a series of hisses, and once you hear it you probably won't forget it. Kitten mortality runs just under 50 percent, as they are preyed upon by owls, hawks, foxes, coyotes, and bears, and are especially vulnerable during the period when they just leave their mother's protection. Adult bobcats will fall prey to larger predators like wolves and mountain lions, with rare instances of black bears and fishers taking full-grown bobcats.

A bobcat will leave a track with four pads clearly defined, without claw marks, as their claws are retractable. The bobcat's tracks are "directly registered" in that they place their rear feet exactly where their front feet fall, so it will appear as though it is walking on two feet. If walking in snow, you may see the edges of the fur around the paw surrounding the track. A bobcat's track will generally measure two inches by two inches, considerably larger than the average house cat.

Bobcat tracks in the sand.

A bobcat will vary its hunting technique according to the size of its prey. With smaller rodents and game animals, it will crouch down and lie in wait until the animals come close by, then pounce on its victim from that position. With larger prey, they will rush in from twenty to thirty feet, chasing their prey much like a leopard or cheetah will. Human predation of bobcats can certainly take its toll on their population, but the bobcat has proven to be resilient, with populations bouncing back quickly. Certainly hunting and trapping can take their toll on bobcat populations, yet the animal's preferred habitat is often so remote that outdoorsmen have less effect on the bobcat population than they do on other species that are more comfortable living near human habitation. Vehicle collisions and secondary poisoning—the consumption of poisoned rodents—are a couple of examples of how humans can have a negative effect on bobcat populations.

My good buddy, Matthew Breuer of Minnesota, specializes in trapping bobcats, and while my own experience is more than limited—due to the lack of a healthy population in the region where I did most of my trapping—I will turn you over to Matthew to share his wisdom and experience in trapping these spotted cats.

"Of all of the critters in all of the biomes in the world, the bobcat has my heart. I love watching them, hunting them, trapping them, seeing them on trail cameras, and so on. I even have a couple of bobcat tattoos. No joke. Their curious nature, yet ninja-like

Breuer's son and a handsome reward for his diligence—a good-size bobcat.

movements, make them so intriguing to me. They are also very difficult to acquire, which probably has heavy weight in my love for them. I'm by no means a cat expert, but I can surely talk about what not to do, and maybe give some insight on what years of trial and error has taught me.

"I've never been a patient person. I live my life in semi-controlled chaos, and waiting for something just isn't my gig. But when it comes to bobcats, if you're not patient you're not going to be successful. I recall a farmer calling me and asking me to take care of a bobcat he had been seeing during muzzle-loader season. He wanted it off of his property, and he had been seeing it daily. He called it a 'slam dunk.' I put out three sets on his property on December 1st, and caught the cat on the second-to-last day of the season, January 2nd. It took almost a month to catch a 'slam dunk.' The farmer wasn't lying; there was sign everywhere. That cat should've been mine on day one. Had it been a fox, I would've collected fur within forty-eight hours. But it wasn't a fox, and it was not a slam dunk. It was like a slow-motion half-court lob that hit the rim six times before slowly slipping through the net. If you take anything away from this section on cat trapping, I hope that the word 'patience' sticks with you."

Bobcat trapping varies greatly in different regions due to ground type, temperature, and general habitat. In the Southwest, you can find cats running cliff edges and rocky ground, where anchoring a trap can be a nightmare. In the North, cat trapping is a winter activity, and snow and ice wreak havoc on sets. A perfectly set snare might be underneath six inches of snow by morning. While each biome has a different way to effectively trap cats; a cat is a cat.

When I say that a cat is a cat, I don't mean that a bobcat is a bobcat . . . I mean a cat is a cat. Bobcats, house cats, barn cats, feral cats . . . they all act similarly. So, if you want to really figure out what makes a bobcat tick, look no further than the cat living in your house or down the street. I would shy away from trying to kidnap the neighbor's cat for research, but you get my drift. I've spent countless hours observing our house and farm cats, trying to pick up on little

Matthew Breuer and his reward for patience.

things that catch their eyes or make them go into predator mode. I've watched them hunt mice and voles in our pasture, and stalk birds near the feeders. I've learned a lot about cat trapping from these observations. The biggest things I've learned are that cats are meticulous, they are very visual, they only hunt when they feel like it, and they are very careful. Keep this in mind as we go forward.

Sets

While there are probably thirty ways to trap a bobcat, I've cut it down to four sets that I've found to be most effective. In talking to several trapping buddies, other nuisance or county trappers, federal trappers, and old-timers, they seem to agree. Snaring, dirt hole sets, walk-through sets, and cubby sets are atop almost every cat trappers list.

Snaring is particularly effective in the North, where snow begins to impede on the travel conditions of even the animals that live there. If you can catch a good track that is consistent, setting a snare can be a great way to put up some fur. Follow the tracks from a distance, meaning don't walk on the tracks. Stay parallel to the tracks until you find a spot that looks like a good pinch point, where a snare can be placed, then come at it from an angle. Disturbing their trails or covering their tracks can be the difference between fur and no fur. I've even spoken with old-timers who carry a small broom and a bobcat's foot to recreate what they find if they disturb the area. They simply brush snow over their tracks, and put a bobcat print on top to make it appear natural. Cats are cautious. They don't like to see things out of place or disturbed. They get nervous, and will turn away. Areas to look for are waterways (especially if frozen), abandoned beaver huts, frozen beaver runs, old clear-cuts, slashings, or anywhere you happen upon sign. Once you've carefully selected spots to hang snares, and have successfully moved in and not disturbed everything, simply hang your snares with an eight- to ten-inch hoop seven to eight inches off of the ground. If you have trouble remembering, you can use the 8x8-inch rule. This works for most cats. If you're snaring in

an area with snow, don't be afraid to push sticks into the snow to guide the cat directly into the snare if you can't find a location that pinches down tight enough. Anchor your snares if you can, but if the ground is frozen and the laws allow, don't be afraid to drill a hole through a small tree to put your wire through. It's simple and very effective. Regulations vary from state-to-state, so be sure to check your local regs before setting snares. Some states require relaxing locks, others allow power snares.

Dirt Hole Sets

Dirt hole sets are obviously the staple in the trapping community. Everyone should be able to make a dirt hole set by the time they are done reading this book. There's no guarantee that you'll make it perfectly, and I promise that no two dirt hole sets will be the same. I screw them up all of the time due to little things like pebbles, roots, not taking my time, etc., but I digress. Dirt hole sets can be very effective when it comes to trapping cats early in the season or in southern states. The two traps I prefer for dirt hole sets are the Minnesota Brand MB-550 and the Bridger #2 Dogless; laminated and offset is preferred. The Bridger #2 Dogless offset laminated is my go-to because of the oversized pan and ease-of-use. They come straight out of the box with an almost flawless night-latch, allowing me to hear the audible "click" when the trap is set perfectly. I like to double swivel my sets, adding a wolf stake if I'm able to lay an anchor in the ground, or I'll attach the trap to my homemade cable tree anchors if the ground is frozen. All connecting parts are held together with s-hooks. My homemade tree anchors are simply a six- to eight-inch length of cable with a small hoop ferruled on one end and a large hoop ferruled on the other. I can simply run the small hoop with the trap around a tree and through the large hoop. This allows me to set a trap anywhere within four to five feet of a tree without having to try to pound in an anchor. I can simply pound the cable into the ground or push it below the snow to hide it.

As you know by now, after digging the trap bed, making is stable and bedded tightly is very important.

If a cat steps on a jaw and it rocks at all, chances are that the cat will boogie. If you're laying footholds down in the snow, wrinkle up wax paper and keep it with you. Place waxed paper in the bottom of the trap bed and over the pan to keep snow from touching the springs. With sun and varying temps, traps will freeze solid in the snow if you don't use something to keep them from doing so. If you're trapping in cold weather without snow, be sure to use peat moss. Peat moss is good and dry, and retains heat to prevent freezing. If you have wax dirt at the ready, use it. If you haven't invested in a two-inch dirt auger that attaches to your cordless drill, you must. Making a dirt hole set becomes painless and speedy with a drill and a dirt auger. Be sure you're setting your trap slightly offset to the hole, and don't be afraid to use sticks or scat to guide the cat's paw onto the pan. Remember, cats are meticulous. They don't like to step on things, and they are very careful with each step they make. I've gone so far that I've put a stick just shy of the back jaw and just in front of the front jaw, hoping the cat steps in the middle. For bait and/or lure, something loud that will last in cold weather is always best. Cats use their sense of smell, but not like canines. It's one of the final senses they use when approaching a set. A few lures that seem to really work well are Caven's Gusto, which has a strong skunk essence, and Milligan's Cat-Man-Do. Both are loud, and long-lasting in the cold. I add bait as well, typically beaver meat, which doesn't freeze as readily as other meats, and is a favorite of cats across the US. Bobcat gland on a piece of scat or the side of the hole works well, and a shot of fox urine on the back of the dirt hole makes it complete . . . almost. What's the sense we're forgetting to appease? Why, it's vision, of course. Always have a visual attractor at cat sets. Even if it's twenty yards away from the set itself, the visual attractor will get them in the area. Shiny objects like silver tinsel or garland work very well, as do wild bird feathers (a turkey wing works wonderfully). I've even heard of people using old CDs or DVDs that shimmer in the moonlight and spin freely when attached to fishing line. Visual attractors are imperative to getting cats near your sets.

Walkthrough Sets

A walkthrough set is very similar to a dirt-hole set, except you're hoping to put a cat's paw on the pan without having it prance around in front of a hole with bait keeping it interested. These sets work especially well if you have an area that you've scouted and have located an active cat trail, but don't have any good places to hang a snare. Using a pinch point or make a pinch point with rocks, sticks, or logs. I use visual attractors directly above the trail I want the cat to use, and I will typically set two traps in the pinch area to double my odds of the cat stepping on a pan. After all, hoping that an animal will step on four inches of earth is a bit of a long shot. Why not make it eight inches? A shot of fox urine and/or bobcat gland along the pinch area is also beneficial. Try to make it look natural, aside from the garland or tinsel of course. Again, be sure to bed your traps tightly, and utilize wax paper, peat moss, or wax dirt if you're trapping in colder climates. In the South, utilizing the homemade tree anchors may work well if you're dealing with rocky or hard ground. The cable even holds well when hooped under large rocks.

Cubby sets can be broken down into two categories; natural and artificial. A natural cubby is made using sticks to make a teepee or utilizing a natural cubby created from a fallen tree. An artificial cubby would include a box or wire cubby that's homemade. Natural cubbies are typical set with a foothold, while artificial cubbies are usually set with a 220 Conibear. Natural cubbies work incredibly well when set correctly, as a cat will feel more comfortable with natural surroundings than it will with a wooden box or a wire cage. With either option, you're going to try to utilize the natural surroundings. Artificial cubbies excel in places like swamps or thickets, where the trap can be hidden and blended into the habitat. Again, a chunk of beaver meat with a call lure is essential, as is a visual attractor. If you want to go a step above and beyond with a cubby, freezing a rabbit carcass with the eyes open works wonders. The light reflects off of the eyes, and you're using their natural prey. Set this right in the cubby and wait. Regardless of which route you go with using a cubby set, try to make it

Curiosity can, indeed, kill the cat.

appear that the cat has a way in and a way out of the cubby. Closed-back cubbies like pails or boxes aren't as effective as wire or natural cubbies that appear to have a way out. Cats don't like to back up, and they don't like feeling trapped (pun intended). Let light shine into the front and back of the cubby. Be sure to check the regs on this one, as Conibear sets are a hot topic, and regulations are ever-changing regarding body-gripping traps, and they vary greatly from state to state.

No matter which type of set you lay down, be prepared to wait. Watch for cold snaps, as cats really like to eat and hunt when the weather turns sour and conditions are tough. During warm stretches, I've seen cats completely leave an area, only to return on the next hard cold snap. A temperature of -25°F with a fresh dusting of snow sounds like a perfect evening for a cat to hunt. It might take eight nights in a row with perfect conditions for your set to be visited, and don't get frustrated if your set is visited

and you don't have a cat. It can take several visits to your set before the cat feels comfortable to actually take that last step.

Catch Care and Catch and Release

If you're lucky enough to catch a bobcat, use caution when approaching it. They have very sharp claws and are extremely fast when they strike. I've had a couple of close calls on lunging cats. If you're comfortable releasing a cat, I highly recommend being selective in the size and sex of the cat you decide to take home. An eighteen-pound female isn't going to sell for a lot of money, and it's not going to make the rug of a lifetime, but it will create more cats for us all to trap in the future.

Taking mature toms is always preferred, but not always possible. Safety is always the number one priority, and if you are using a Conibear, there's obviously no releasing the cat. Once you have your trophy in possession, take your time in skinning, as bobcats are

While smaller than what you would want to take, this bobcat was feeding on livestock, and had to go.

one of the better furs on the market. Be sure to register and tag your animal if your state requires it. Take a lot of photos . . . they are truly beautiful animals.

Fisher—The Cat That Isn't

Though it may look like a feline, the fisher is related to the weasel family.

In the northern boreal forests, ranging in an arc from the White Mountains of New Hampshire, the Green Mountains of Vermont, and New York's Adirondacks northerly into middle latitudes of central Canada and back down into the Pacific Northwest, lives the fisher. A solitary, unique animal, the fisher—also known as the fisher cat—neither fishes, nor is it a cat. What it is, is a carnivorous, furbearing mammal, related to the marten, with the males measuring three to four feet in length, and weighing between eight and thirteen pounds, which can be rather imposing when encountered in the wild.

The fisher—*Pekania pennant*—is predominately a predator, feeding primarily on snowshoe hares, cottontail rabbits, and porcupines, though they will take smaller rodents, fruits, nuts, berries, and insects, and aren't ashamed to eat carrion during pressing times. The fisher is dimorphic, and the males are nearly twice the size of the females. They are long, sleek, and low to the ground, with excellent dexterity; a fisher is equally at home in trees as it is travelling along the ground. They have a dark brown, coarse fur that will vary from one to three inches thick on their back. The face and neck of a fisher will be a bit lighter in color than the body, sometimes with gold highlights. Their fur will change color throughout the seasons, with the summer coat being much lighter (sometimes with white or cream colored patches) than the winter coat.

The fisher is a ferocious little bugger. (Photo Credit: Getty Images.)

The fisher has five toes on each foot, replete with non-retractable claws. Their feet are wide—helping the fisher stay on top of the snow in winter—and the fisher has specialized ankles that greatly aid in climbing and descending trees. As a matter of fact, the fisher is one of the few mammals that can descend a tree head first. Throughout the year, the fisher is a rather solitary creature, seeking out one another but once a year for mating. And the physiological process of reproduction in the fisher is a very interesting one.

The males and females will couple at some point late in late March or early April, when the actual

A fisher creeping through the forest. (Photo Credit: Getty Images.)

insemination occurs, but the female fisher's body goes into a "dormant pregnancy" for ten or eleven months. Somehow, gestation doesn't begin until the following February, when she will carry her young for fifty days, giving birth to one to four kits. Ten days after giving birth, the female will once again come into estrus, and the cycle will start over. The kits will only stay with their mother for four or five months. After that, they will be expelled to claim their own home range, and begin breeding by their first birthday.

The fisher is crepuscular, active just before and after dusk and dawn respectively, as well as throughout the night. They do not hibernate, instead remaining active throughout even the coldest winter months. Depending on the season, a fisher will have a vast home range, from three square miles in the summer to up to (sometimes over) five square miles during the winter. Whether this is a natural tendency, or their range needs to be that large because they inhabit those forests where the game density is

seriously low, is not known, but understand the fisher enjoys the solitude of the wilds. One possibility is that the females need a hollow tree or log in order to make a nest for their young, and only an old-growth forest can routinely provide those scenarios. They not only prefer solitude, but prefer to live in those forests with a heavy canopy—hence the preference for the Northeast's desolate, ancient forests—and will shun the more open, younger forests where the canopy is open.

Fishers are courageous animals, routinely feeding on porcupines. They will circle the quill pig until they can bite it in the face repeatedly. This process may take as long as a half an hour, but the diligent fisher doesn't quit. Couple this bravado with the huge area that a fisher will cover, and a trapper can use these characteristics to his or her advantage.

A fisher's fur is highly desirable; it has historically brought one of the highest per pelt prices of all the furbearers. While the fisher's range is limited (in comparison to many other furbearers), if you find evidence of the presence of fishers in your area, making a couple of sets for them will be well worth the effort. Prepare yourself for some hiking, as well as time in the desolate forests that I love so much.

The pine marten is similar to the fisher, yet smaller. They inhabit the North Country, from the northern Adirondacks of my native New York, along the US/Canada border states, and up into northern Canada and Alaska. They are curious creatures, and I've often had them investigate bear bait sites, from Alaska to Quebec. They—like the fisher—are creatures of the deep, solitary forests.

While I make several hunting trips to the remote woods of the North each year, I don't trap there, as it's quite far from home. However, my buddy Matthew

Breuer lives in the Minnesota North Country, and has many more opportunities to trap this pair of predators, so once again I'll defer to his knowledge.

Fisher tracks in the snow.

Trapping Fisher (and the Pine Marten)—Matthew Breuer

While fisher and pine marten are different, they are very much the same. They are both big, mean, curious weasels, ferocious predators that are hardly seen or heard. Both can be trapped in a similar manner, but the areas they can be found in often differ. There's definitely some overlap in cedar swamps, and the large pine forests near the Canadian Shield are a prime example of the two species cohabitating. Fishers often prefer mixed forests, as they love to nest and den in large holes or hollow oak trees. Fallen timber snags and uprooted trees also appeal to both species. Fisher and marten regulations vary greatly from state-to-state, so be sure you're checking on the regulations for the area you'll be trapping. For us trappers in Minnesota, you can have a total of two marten and/or fisher; meaning two fisher, two marten, or one of each. Our season is only five days long, so being prepared when opening day rolls around is imperative. Pre-baiting areas can be effective, and trail cameras are a great tool for scouting out possible areas. Once you locate marten or fisher, trapping them is typically not that difficult.

Sets

The most popular way to catch marten and fisher is with the use of Conibears; 160 or 220 for fisher, and 160 for marten. There are two effective ways to target each species with Conibears. The first way is to use a box set, or cubby set. Making a cubby for either species is relatively easy. Form an open-ended rectangular box, leaving both ends open. Use chicken wire to close it off the back side. This gives the weasel a comforting feeling, thinking it won't be walking into a hole it will have to back out of. It also allows for better scent dispersion, which is good, considering how much weasels rely on their noses to feed. If you don't want to build a box, an old mailbox works well for pine marten, especially in or on trees. Baiting the set with a variety of meat, from duck carcasses to deer scraps or beaver meat, works well. Beaver meat is preferred. Adding some Lenon's All Call lure or something skunky like Gusto to the box will help pull critters from a distance. In the front of the box, cut out notches for the springs and simply place the Conibear in the front opening. I like to bend my triggers out a bit, hoping to not impede the visual for the weasel. Even bending one trigger away and leaving one down works well. Set your box on the ground and cover it in pine boughs, with enough hanging over the top edge to catch any snow that may fall. Lifting the front end of the box with a branch or small log helps, too. This keeps the snow from blocking the entrance. Or, wire the box on a tree or large stump.

Another very good set for fisher and marten is the leaning pole set. It's simple, very effective, and light to carry in. A lot of leaning-pole sets can be made in a day, compared to cubby sets, which can be heavy and cumbersome. Simply find a leaning tree, or lean a fallen tree against a different tree, use a Conibear stabilizer to hold your Conibear to the leaning pole, set the trap, wire bait to the pole above the trap, then cover the bait from the top end with pine boughs. I like to add pine to the trap edges as well, making it appear more natural. Again, beaver meat is preferred, and a call lure helps, but any chunk of meat will work. Fisher cats and pine marten are both tree climbers, and will read-

Matthew Breuer with a hard-earned fisher.

ily climb a pole or a straight tree if they are after food. This is especially true in the winter, when both species spend mountains of time in the trees when the snow cover is high.

Other types of sets can work as well. I've caught fisher in gray fox foothold sets using sweet smells for lure. I've also seen fisher and marten caught in live traps. Both species are very curious, which makes them relatively easy to catch. The tricky part is finding them, and having them stick around long enough to catch them. Both species cover large areas, and aren't as abundant as their smaller weasel cousins. Catching a prime fisher or pine marten is truly rewarding, as they are incredible creatures sporting beautiful fur.

Muskrat

The muskrat, *Ondatra zibethicus*, is a semi-aquatic rodent, widely distributed across North America—excluding Mexico and the extreme northern climes—and also across northern Europe, where it was introduced. This mischievous little fellow inhabits numerous ponds, lakes, streams, and other bodies of water, building its houses in a tell-tale fashion; the cone-shaped dwellings—also known as push-ups—are constructed of sticks, twigs, reeds, and any other materials readily available, rising two to four feet above the waterline. These muskrats are

also known to excavate and dwell in holes in the banks of streams, lakes, and ponds. Each muskrat home will have at least two, and sometimes up to seven or eight, entrances. They have been known to eradicate certain species of vegetation in wetland areas.

The muskrat will avoid eating the purple loosestrife plants whenever possible, allowing the invasive plant to spread throughout wetlands, replacing the cattail that the muskrat enjoys so much. Muskrats prefer to feed in water, and do not store food for the winter, instead actually feeding on the very materials

A muskrat, on the front porch of its house.

A muskrat house or push-up, in the middle of a pond.

that comprise their push-ups when food becomes scarce.

The muskrat is a fur-covered rodent, red-brown to dark brown (and sometimes approaching black) in color.

They will weigh one and one-half to four and one-half pounds in extreme cases, measuring anywhere from sixteen to twenty-eight inches in length, including the tail, which is leaf-shaped in cross section, devoid of fur, with a leathery, almost scaly appearance, which they drag along the ground when walking on the shore, making a distinct and easy-to-recognize track. Their short front feet have long, sharp nails, and the larger rear feet are partially webbed. The muskrat is a diurnal animal, with prevalent activity near sunrise and sunset. The muskrat is an omnivore, though he feeds predominately on vegetation. Cattails, rice grass, and the roots of numerous plants are the muskrat's chosen fare, though leaves, corn, grasses, and freshwater mussels are also on the menu.

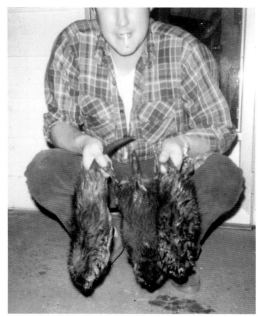

Philip J. Massaro with a trio of muskrats in the late 1970s; the 'rat on the right is nearly black in color.

Muskrats generally begin breeding in March and April, with a one-month gestation period, and litters up to one dozen young are not uncommon. They may have two to four litters annually, making for frequent population explosions, though the actual population numbers are subject to a cyclical rise and decline. Their spread—which can be detrimental to sensitive wetlands—can be kept in check through trapping. Mink will feed on muskrat, as will birds of prey, with foxes and coyotes taking them as a target of opportunity.

Muskrat fur has long been prized for its warmth, being fashioned into hats and coats. The Royal Canadian Mounted Police are issued winter hats made of muskrat fur.

Trapping Equipment and Techniques

Finding muskrat is no great endeavor; there are several tell-tale signs that muskrats are present. However, pre-season scouting will definitely make or break your trapping season. Look to the water for the easy-to-spot muskrat push-ups, keeping your eyes on the shoreline for their tracks—with the definitive tail marks in the middle—and for the muskrat "highways" in the shallows, which muskrats use to travel

A muskrat trail from shore toward its house or push-up.

to and from their houses. Scat on exposed rocks, stumps, and partially submerged logs is also evidence of muskrat activity.

The drown set was the predominant means of trapping muskrat, although in recent years the #110 and #120 Conibear traps account for the majority of muskrats taken. Traps set below the waterline along the shore or near exposed areas above water where muskrat frequent (i.e., rocks, stumps, grass hillocks) will not only effectively take muskrat, but mink and raccoon as well. There are several techniques which will effectively take muskrat, and we'll get into greater detail momentarily. Single long-spring traps—#1½, to be specific—are perfect for muskrat trapping, as are #1½ double coil and #1½ jump traps. All three will hold raccoon and mink as well.

An Oneida Victor No. 1½ stop-loss trap, perfect for muskrats.

For scents, there are several types of gland (musk) lures and food lures that will work for muskrat, as well as the aforementioned mink and raccoon. They may be used independently, or in conjunction, depending on the set. It's very possible to come up with your own home-brew, but for the beginner, or those with time restraints, there are many great lures on the market that will suffice. Murray's, Dobbins, and S. Stanley Hawbaker & Sons all offer tried-and-true formulae for the trapper.

Muskrat trap preparation is as outlined earlier in this book, but the Conibear traps are not customarily waxed. We have waxed Conibears in the past—greatly increasing the speed of the trap closure—to keep them as rust free as possible, but it is not necessary to do so. Should you choose to wax your Conibear traps, take extra care and time when setting your traps, using a knife to remove all the wax from the area where the trigger, dog, and the jaw meet, as well as removing wax from the bottom portion

Philip P. Massaro examining muskrat runs in the early winter.

Muskrat tracks on the muddy shore; note the tail being dragged along in the center.

of the dog. This will help prevent accidental release, and keep your fingers in their current anatomical arrangement.

Let's now take a look at several popular sets to take muskrat. Most of these have a very good chance at taking mink and raccoon as well.

A Favorite for Muskrat

One of my favorite set for muskrats in ponds, lakes, and swamps was designed around the #110 and#120 Conibear, placed along the numerous "highways"—those submerged trails or paths on the bottom of the ponds or lakes. The idea is simple: A muskrat, normally traveling these highways, will swim through a Conibear trap and be dispatched instantly. I've set multiple traps along a single trail—usually the one most frequently used—roughly eight to ten feet apart, and have had multiple catches in the same evening. While this sounds relatively simple, it is very effective and productive, as it uses the animal's natural movements and travels to direct it into the trap. A simple stake—say one inch or slightly larger—is all that is needed to hold the Conibear in place, as the muskrat will be dead quickly, and there's really no risk of larger animals getting into this set. I would advise against using this set-up in areas where beavers may be present, as the #110 and #120 aren't sufficient to dispatch a beaver.

The Float Set

This is a very effective set, especially in bodies of water where rising and falling water levels pose an issue, but also works well in those places where the water level is constant. The float set works on the concept that muskrats will readily climb up on floating logs and other debris in the water, away from shore, where they enjoy the safety of isolation from mink, coyotes, and foxes. This set works well if you can place it before season (obviously without traps attached) so

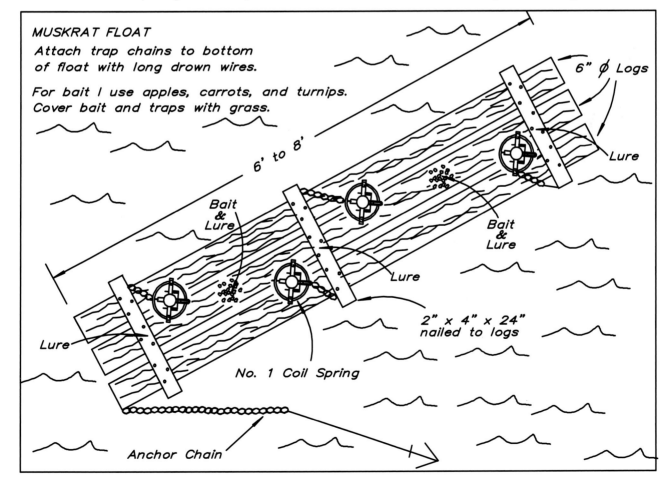

MUSKRAT FLOAT
Attach trap chains to bottom of float with long drown wires.

For bait I use apples, carrots, and turnips. Cover bait and traps with grass.

6" ∅ Logs

6' to 8'

Lure

Bait & Lure

Bait & Lure

Lure

2" x 4" x 24" nailed to logs

Lure

No. 1 Coil Spring

Lure

Anchor Chain

the muskrats can become accustomed to the presence of the float.

The preparation is relatively easy. Using at least two logs—roughly six inches in diameter and at least eight feet in length—scabbed together with some smaller two-inch diameter branches, notch out two or three flat areas along the junction of the two logs big enough to hold a #1½ jump- or coil-spring trap. The trap chains are then wired underneath the float set, to secure the muskrat to the logs once dispatched. Traps should be bedded in and covered with soupy mud and leaves, as well as fine grass cuttings. You may weight the trap wire to ensure quick death, though the very weight of the trap itself should suffice. In a pond or lake, you may simply anchor the float set anywhere, but in bodies of water with varying water elevations, be sure and anchor your float set to a tree or limb above the water surface to prevent submerging the float set as the water rises.

A few drops of gland or food lure, placed between the traps, will help to draw the muskrats onto the float and into the traps, but lure is not an absolute necessity.

The Pipe or Drain Set

Drain pipes that empty into a body water or drainage ditches are favorite places for muskrats to explore, and therefore offer excellent opportunities for a trapper to catch them. There are several possible scenarios, each of which requires a different approach.

If the drain pipe is nearly or fully submerged, a #110 or #120 Conibear, placed four inches out from the pipe's end, and secured to a stake on the bank, or staked to the bottom will produce results. If the pipe is not submerged, a #1½ trap, placed on a flat rock two to three inches under the surface of the water—about three inches from the end of the pipe—will not only produce muskrats, but give you a good chance at both mink and raccoon as well. Cover your trap with fine mud or sand.

American Mink: *Neovison Vison*

American mink are native to North America; their range is as far south as Florida and as far north as northern Alaska and Canada, with very few mink being present in our southern border states. They have been introduced to Europe and South America mostly through fur farming. Their closest relative is the Siberian weasel. They are a semi-aquatic animal, with webbing between their digits. They are, by far, the most frequently farmed animal for their fur, prized for its appearance and texture.

They are, for the most part, carnivorous. They prey on all kinds of rodents, fish, crustaceans, frogs,

The quick-witted and agile mink. (Photo Credit: Getty Images.)

Mink love to eat fish. (Photo Credit: Getty Images.)

birds, and chickens (they can clean out a hen house quickly). They are experts in hunting and killing muskrats, which is one of their favorite meals.

The adult male mink is larger in size than the female, weighing from one to three pounds, its body measuring twelve to twenty inches in length, with a tail measuring from six to ten inches long. Adult females weigh from one to two pounds, their body measuring twelve to fifteen inches in length, with a tail measuring from six to eight inches long. Their fur ranges from light brown to dark brown in color, depending on the time of year, being lighter in summer. They have a thick, soft underfur and oily guard-hairs which are water resistant. Their fur is used for coats, jackets, stoles, capes, and trim.

Mink can travel up to four miles per hour over land and are great swimmers.

They rarely dive deeper than about one foot under the water while foraging and hunting for prey like fish and muskrats. When hunting, mink will rely on their sight, though they have an exultant sense of hearing. Their sense of smell is considered weak.

Mink have two anal glands for marking territory and leaving their scent for mating. It has a very strong and obnoxious odor, almost nauseating to humans. Mink can carry some diseases that can be transferred to cattle and sheep. Mink have a breeding season of about three weeks long, starting in February in the southern parts of their range to April in the northern parts of their range. Females will mate with multiple males, having litters of four kits on average, which are born from April to June and weigh about six grams each. Litters of up to sixteen have been recorded from mink raised in captivity. Female mink usually pick an old muskrat den or hollow log in which to give birth and raise their young. The kits are born blind, completely dependent on their mother's milk. Their eyes open in about twenty-five days and are weaned at about five weeks of age. They start hunting with their mother at about eight weeks of age (the males take no part in raising the young), and the kits stay with their mother until the fall dispersal. Kits are very vocal and squeak loudly when separated from their mother. Mink attain full maturity and are able to breed at about ten months of age. A mink's range is between one to three miles, with the males ranging farther out than the females, probably due to the males' quest for females during breeding season.

Fish and muskrats are their primary prey, but being excellent climbers, mink can take squirrels and birds when the opportunity presents itself.

Mink travel well across both land and water.

The mink is an efficient predator; note the sharp canine teeth.

They are masters of killing muskrats on dry land and shallow water, and are the muskrat's biggest problem in their everyday life activities. Mink do not hibernate, making them available to be trapped throughout the entire trapping season. When actively foraging and hunting, a mink will scamper and swim, going in and out of the water, investigating every drain pipe, drainage ditch, those tree roots half-in and half-out of the water along the shore of a stream, and every pocket and burrow they come across. Keep this in the forefront of your mind when scouting before season opens and when working your trap line.

Traps

The leghold trap that I most favor for mink is the No. 1½ double-coil spring. I favor this trap over the No. 1½ long spring or double long spring because it takes up less room in my trap basket, it is much easier to conceal, it is a faster and stronger trap in my view, and it will fit handily within some sets where long springs will require additional work to excavate the set properly. The No. 1 double coil will work just as well for mink, but there is usually always a possibility of catching a raccoon at a baited mink set, and I feel the No.1 is a little light to hold a large raccoon. The pan tension on the traps should be set very loose, so that the pan will flop up or down just from the weight of the pan itself, but not wobble left or right. Traps should be dyed and waxed, not so much to be scent-free but to protect the trap from the elements. The No. 110 and No. 120 Conibear are in my opinion the best size body-gripping traps for mink sets. For any baited set using a body-gripping trap,

An Oneida Victor No. 1 coil-spring trap, a good choice for mink.

where the trap is not totally submerged, I prefer the No. 120, as it will dispatch any raccoon that happens along. Anchor all body-gripping traps well to prevent them from being washed away with your catch from rising flood waters, as conditions can change rapidly. All leghold traps should have extra-long chains or wire attached to anchor them well, as the weight of the leghold trap may also drown the mink, providing the chain or wire is long enough to allow the animal to get into deeper water.

Lure and Bait

The only lure that I personally use for mink sets is a mink gland lure, which I purchase from trapping supply houses. As for bait, a fresh piece of fish is my favorite, closely followed by fresh muskrat meat. I usually make my own fish-based bait (formed into a paste for ease of use) just before season. I will give you the recipe, which was given to me by my friend and an excellent trapper, the late Joe Moskaluk, for a great mink and muskrat bait. You can easily make it yourself from items available from your grocery store.

This bait will also take raccoons and, if used in a dirt hole set, I have even caught gray fox with it. I had run out of bait one time while setting for fox, and this was the only bait I had left to use. I did not expect to catch a fox, but rather a raccoon, but I figured it was better than nothing, and to my surprise, it worked. There are many mink baits (both fish-based and meat-based) on the market today that will work well. I can honestly say this recipe has worked just as well for me as the baits I have purchased in the past. You may want to prepare it outdoors, as it has the potential to stink up a kitchen very fast.

Fish-Based Mink Bait

1 can of mackerel or herring
2 cans of sardines, the cheaper the better
1 can of oysters
3 tablespoons of vegetable or canola oil.
3 tablespoons of glycerin
1 box of corn starch (If you don't have corn starch, you can substitute flour.)

Wearing a pair of clean latex or rubber gloves, in a clean mixing bowl empty the entire contents, juice and all, of the canned mackerel or herring. Using a large fork, chop and mash the fish as best you can. Next add in your sardines and oysters, again the entire contents of each can. Mash them into the fish and mix together thoroughly. Add in your three tablespoons of vegetable or canola oil. Mix this soupy mixture until all is blended together. Now add your three tablespoons of glycerin and mix until totally blended. Next—while constantly stirring—add the corn starch, a little at a time until the fishy mixture becomes the consistency of toothpaste or cookie dough. This bait is very pungent, and only about a teaspoon is required at each set to be effective. I usually place this bait on a wad of grass or small piece of bark before placing it where I want it at the set.

← 1³/₈ in. →

front

↕ 1³/₄ in.

hind

Mink tracks.

Sets

Before we get going, the first thing I want to tell you is that a good pair of hip boots will be invaluable, especially when trapping mink and muskrats. When you obtain a pair, take extra care not to puncture or tear them, especially when crossing wire fences. There is nothing more annoying or frustrating than a leaky pair of hip boots, as sets for mink will invariably be near the water.

The Pocket Set (non-pipe)

The pocket set is the set I was first successful with when I was still trying to catch my first mink, once somebody showed me how to construct it correctly. At that time I did not have access to any trapping books (and there was no such thing as the Internet, let alone computers), so when an experienced trapper is willing to show how to make any set, whether you intend to use it at the time or not, do not turn down the opportunity; you can always learn something that may come in handy at a later date. If opportunity knocks, answer the door!

The pocket set in my opinion is the best baited and non-baited set for mink. It uses the instinctive habit a mink has of investigating every hole, pocket, and drain pipe along a stream. I have caught mink with merely a muskrat gland lure placed up and in the back of an abandoned muskrat hole. We can improve the odds in our favor by adding a bait, lure, and a well-placed trap to the mix. The majority of my pocket sets consist of a leghold trap, rigged up for a drown set, if the water is deep enough. I like drown sets because not only will they hide the captured mink from the eyes of potential thieves, but a live mink in a trap is a ferocious animal. If the mink is drowned, there is no damage whatsoever to the pelt and no confrontation at the set. For my pocket sets, I pick a spot along the bank of a stream where there is a point of land, large or very small, that protrudes off the bank, especially if it is located at a bend in the stream. This set is much easier to construct if the stream bed is fairly flat right up to the bank. If it drops off too quickly you may have to place a flat rock under your trap to get it level and at the correct depth. Have your trap set before you approach the site. While standing in the water facing the bank, dig a four-inch-diameter hole into the bank so the bottom of the hole is right at the water level. Dig the hole at right angles to the bank, at a 30- to 45-degree upward slant. Make your hole at least a foot in length. With your tool or gloved hand, make a little flat shelf in the back of the hole. Next place your bait on the small shelf you just constructed and rinse your hands off in the stream. Next, dig out a flat area at the mouth of the hole and a short distance into the hole, just wide enough to accept your trap and deep enough so that when you place your trap, the pan is one-half

This natural cubby—a pocket in a stone wall—is a good choice for a mink set.

to three-quarters of an inch below the water. Some water should be allowed to flow into the hole. Mink have very short legs and you do not want the mink to swim right over the pan without triggering it. Place some mink gland lure at the top edge of the entrance of your pocket. You can camouflage the trap with some mud, making sure there is no debris that will clog the trap when triggered. Stake your trap with the long chain or wire so that the trapped mink has access to deep water, deep enough to drown him. Exit the set through the water for a few steps, leaving no human scent at the set. This set should be good for at least a week, not needing any re-baiting for that period of time. The only thing that may need attention is the depth of the trap, due to rising and falling water levels. Always check your set by approaching it in the water if possible.

If the stream is so shallow that a drown set is impossible, you can substitute a No. 110 or No. 120 Conibear. It involves a little more work, but will work just as well. What I do is construct the pocket or tunnel as instructed above. At the mouth of the hole I dig the bottom out a little deeper and farther into the pocket, allowing a short portion of the pocket or tunnel to flood. I set the body-gripping trap (when set and ready) in place, so that the top of the trap is level with the top of the entrance. If constructed properly, three-quarters of the trap body should be under water. I conceal the exposed portion of the trap with grass and mud so the trap looks like the trap is part of the pocket or tunnel. Anchor the body-gripping trap well, so it cannot be washed away by the current or rising flood waters.

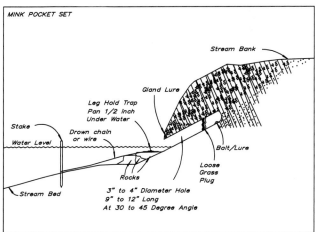

Good mink country, this stream is certainly a place to look for mink sign.

Pocket Set (with pipe)

The same set described above can also be accomplished by using a fifteen-inch-long piece of four-inch-diameter PVC plastic pipe. Instead of digging your pocket, you dig out a larger hole in the bank of the stream, and install the length of PVC pipe. This set will work well, but it has a few drawbacks. The first is that it is much more time consuming to install, which almost forces you to install it long before the trapping season starts. Second, you have no way of knowing what the water level will be that far in advance and all your work could possibly have been in vain. And third, they are much more visible. People such as fishermen, hunters, and hikers can see them and could return during trapping season to retrieve your catch, traps and all. Another thought to keep in mind is that you may not have permission the following year to trap that section of stream, and all your hard work was wasted.

The Funnel Set

Mink will travel up and down every run of water no matter how small. There are numerous small feeder streams and drainage ditches that have flowing water in them throughout the fall of the year. Some may be only be one-foot wide and some a little larger. These small runs of water are great places for a funnel set. The outflow ditches from swamps or ponds are ideal. What you do is construct a narrow channel with stones or logs in the water. It can be as short as a foot

Philip J. Massaro indicates a good mink run, and a place for a set.

in length. At the downstream end of this constriction or funnel, place your trap so that there is about three-quarters of an inch of water over the pan. You can enhance this set by placing a few drops of mink gland lure on a rock or log right to the left or right of the trap. You can use a body-gripping trap if you prefer by placing it midway in the channel so that the mink is forced to swim through the trap. If using a body-gripping trap, I usually make the narrow channel a little longer, two to three feet in length.

Feeder Stream Sets

Place these where feeder streams and ditches empty into a larger stream—the narrower the feeder stream or ditch, the better. Mink explore these intersections regularly. What I like to do is this: In the center of the feeder stream or ditch, in line with the edge or bank of the stream it is emptying into, I drive a stake or tree limb about an inch or two in diameter into the bed of the ditch or stream, so it sticks out of the water about a foot or more.

The authors discussing a set on a feeder stream.

I attach my leghold trap to the stake. I set the trap right up next to the stake, almost touching. The trap should be set so there is about an inch of water over the pan. If the water is too deep, use a flat rock or two to achieve this. If the water is too shallow, dig out the stream bed a little to accomplish the desired depth. Now I smear a few drops of mink gland lure on the face of the stake facing the trap, about six inches above the water.

A perfect hollow log for a mink set.

Hollow Log Set

If you come across a hollow log, in or near a stream, place it up against the bank so about two to three inches of water is running right through it. The hole in the log should be six inches or larger in diameter.

You can also use a short length of six-inch-diameter PVC plastic pipe that you can place before season so the mink will get used to going through it. I like to cover the log or pipe with rocks and debris. Place a trap at each end of the log, with about one inch of water over the pan. Place a few drops of gland lure on the top edge of the entrances of the log at both ends. You may have to place a small, very flat rock on the downstream side of each trap to stop the current from moving your trap. On very large hollow logs—those with openings ten inches or larger in diameter—use a stone on one side of the opening to guide the mink into your trap.

Undercut Bank Sets

Many times you will find streams whose banks are undercut. These are mink highways; you can easily place some natural debris up against the undercut bank, creating a natural tunnel about six inches in diameter. These can also be built during the offseason so they are regularly traveled by trapping season. You can look for mink tracks in the mud or snow to see if the mink are using it. Place a concealed, staked trap at one end of the tunnel. If there is water running through your tunnel, all the better. No bait is to be used at this set, though a few drops of gland lure placed in the middle of the tunnel, at the top or on the side, should improve your chances of a catch.

Places where nature has washed away the soil around the roots of a tree growing on the bank of the stream, and created semi-covered arched passageway, allowing the water to flow through, are great spots for mink sets. Again, you may have to place a flat rock or two to set your trap on, so there is one inch of water flowing over the trap pan. Place a few drops of gland lure on the root right above your trap. You can tie off your trap to the roots as well. This is also a good spot to use a body-gripping trap. If using a body-gripping trap, use no lure, as you want the mink to swim right through your trap.

Culvert Set

Culverts going under roads are very good places for mink sets. Most furbearers use culverts to cross roads (as opposed to going over them). Culverts are not only used for travel, but most of the time there are small pools at the ends of the them which harbor frogs, minnows, and the like. They are like a giant funnel for not only mink but for raccoons and musk-rats as well. At culvert sets for mink, you want to anchor your traps as if you were prepared to catch a large raccoon, as well you might. Place your leg-hold trap about six inches inside the culvert. Place a flat stone that does not protrude out of the water on the downstream side of the trap. If you are going to place only one trap, on one end of the culvert, place it on the downstream end of the culvert. Culverts are also good places for sets because you can check them quickly and you can cover a lot of territory by vehicle. Another positive attribute to these sets is that your catch is well hidden from plain sight, as the catch will normally hide inside the culvert.

When checking the culvert sets by vehicle, spend as little time as possible, and do not park right at the culvert, as passersby will notice you after a few days and figure out what you are doing; you certainly do not need a new partner.

A Dry Land Set

The best dry land set for mink that I know of is very similar to the dirt-hole set for foxes. There are a few minor differences that I will point out. Location of the set should be only a few feet off a trail used by mink. The top of tall banks along a stream with an obvious narrow trail, running parallel with the stream, is a good example. No bait is used at this set, just a good mink lure. You can make this dirt hole up against a log or stone. Dig out a trap bed just big enough to conceal your trap and stake, no bigger. Your bait hole, which

is to be dug at about 45 degrees, should be no larger than three inches in diameter, and about nine to twelve inches deep. Use a clean, dyed, and waxed No. 1½ or No.2 coil-spring trap. Bed the trap very close to the hole, so that the jaw is just touching the edge of the hole, but concealed. Once bedded, the trap should only be covered with half an inch of dirt, no more. Your pan tension should be reduced to zero. In other words, when the trap is not set, the pan should move freely up and down by its own weight, but not wobble left or right. Trap pan should be set on a hair trigger. Use a pan cover, do not block the pan. Place a good mink lure down the bait hole, and a mink gland lure on the top edge of the hole. Use extreme care not to leave any human scent at the set, as you would with a fox set.

Mink Boxes (Non-Floating)

There are so many types and designs of mink boxes that you could write a book about them. There are floating and non-floating types. The floating types are more sophisticated, take longer to build, and are more difficult to deploy. I will attempt to tell you how construct a non-floating mink box that I think will work best and last for seasons. It can be made out of scrap lumber, carried relatively easily, and concealed from sight with just a little material found on site. Construct a box so that the inside dimensions of the opening are seven inches by seven inches. This box should be a minimum of twelve inches long, though eighteen inches would be better. Attach the sides to the top and bottom with finishing nails and glue or just screws alone. On the side panels, cut a one-inch-wide slot centered between the top and bottom, four inches long to accept your body-gripping trap springs.

The fastest way to make your spring slots is to drill a one-inch-diameter hole four inches back from the front end, exactly centered on the side panel board. Then you can cut the slots from the front end of the side panel to the hole. Cut out these slots before you assemble your box. I use a No. 120 Conibear trap for this box. The back end of your box will be covered by stapling a quarter-inch mesh square panel. The reason for wire mesh as opposed to just closing it off with wood is to allow the scent of the bait or lure to escape.

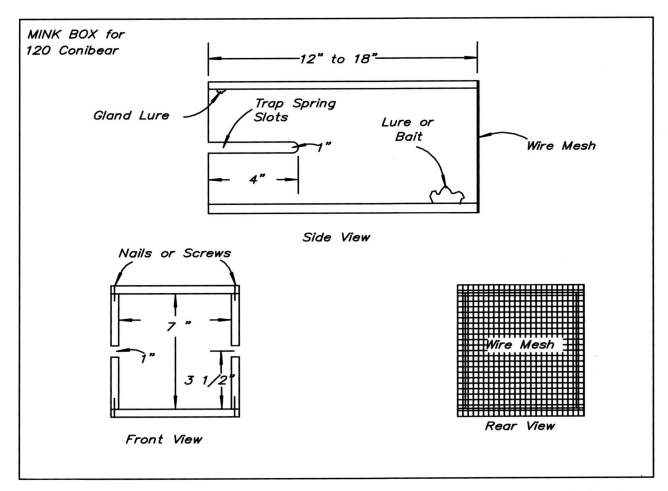

MINK BOX for
120 Conibear

12" to 18"

Gland Lure

Trap Spring
Slots

1"

4"

Lure or
Bait

Wire Mesh

Side View

Nails or Screws

7"

1"

3 1/2"

Front View

Wire Mesh

Rear View

When completed, you can spray paint the outside of the box camouflage. Some trappers drill an additional hole in the side of the box to wire the trap to. I like to tie off the trap to an independent, more stable object, such as a driven stake or sapling. The reason for this is that if you get a larger catch, like a large raccoon, and it is not killed, it can carry off box and all. When placing these boxes, I go through great pains to cover them with local material. The below diagram will be most helpful in constructing your mink box.

Beaver — Builder of Dams

The North American beaver—*Castor canadensis*—is the furbearing mammal most responsible for the trapping craze that led to the exploration and eventual settling of much of North America. Its fur was the prime target of those rugged mountain men and fur trappers, as the short, thick fur underneath the guardhairs are absolutely perfect for shearing, and

The bucktoothed beaver, chewer of trees. (Photo Credit: Getty Images.)

making the felt necessary for the hats that were in vogue throughout Europe from the 1500s until the mid-1800s. They are found all across North America, from northern Canada to southern Mexico, coast to coast.

The beaver is an interesting animal, being one of the few creatures on earth—along with man—who creates its own habitat. A beaver will spend its life as a dam engineer, creating a series of dams along a stream, building its lodge within the pool which results from the dam. As the beavers reproduce, the young adults are usually expelled from the lodge at age two and will head both upstream and downstream, to create dams and houses of their own. The lodge will be clearly evident, looking like a raised mound of sticks in the middle of the dammed pool. The entrance to the lodge will be underwater, and a room will be constructed above the waterline, where the beaver will spend the winter, not quite in a state of hibernation, but limiting activity during the coldest and darkest periods.

The beaver must chew throughout its life to keep its teeth worn to an acceptable level. (Photo Credit: Getty Images.)

Beaver have reddish-brown colored fur, with some examples nearly black. The beaver is equipped with a large set of incisors—protected by a thick layer of orange enamel—which will grow throughout its life; the beaver must chew wood to keep the incisors worn down, or they will grow around the jaw, killing the animal. So they will chew and chew, predominately on soft wood like alder, poplar, and willow, though I seldom have seen beavers chew oak trees. When you see signs of beavers starting to chew on hardwood trees, they have used up the majority of their natural feed, and will be moving on to greener pastures soon. The two sets of teeth are self-sharpening. Beavers live on the bark of the trees and

limbs they fell—and some soft vegetation like water lilies in the spring—and use the logs, branches, and twigs to construct their dams, packing the intertwined frame with mud and weeds. The resultant pool protects the beaver from predators, and the seclusion of the beaver house allows the animal to raise its young in safety.

The beaver's webbed rear feet and broad, leathery tail aid in both swimming and the beaver's signature alarm signal: it will use that flat tail to slap the water loudly, and once you hear a beaver's alarm, you'll remember it. My first encounter with this alarm call came in Quebec, Canada while I was hunting moose. There was a long, narrow beaver pond, edged with willow—that the moose love to feed on—and I crept up as silently as possible to pick a stand from which to call moose. The beaver and I had no idea the other was there, but once it sensed me, it gave that loud slap literally right at my feet. Both of us escaped unharmed, but it did scare the pants off me! Once a beaver sounds the alarm, the other beavers in the colony will stay submerged for some time.

It is easy to find the sign of a beaver; there will be chewed stumps and half-chewed trees, and peeled sticks surrounding the shoreline of the beaver's home. There will be "slides" along the shore where the beaver drags the logs and branches into the water to build its homes and dams. These slides can be used to the trapper's advantage, as you'll soon see.

The beaver's genus—castor—is derived from the

The tell-tale chewing signs of the beaver.

castor glands at the base of the tail, which the beaver uses in addition to its urine as a marking scent. This castor has played an important role in the production of perfumes, offering a leathery smell. It has also been used as a food additive, as well as for flavoring liquor. The odor of beaver castor is rather pungent, and can be used to bait your beaver traps.

Beaver castor is harvested and sold by trappers. Beaver castor is not only used in beaver lure, but is an ingredient in most all other lures, like mink, fox, bobcat, coyote, raccoon . . . this list goes on and on. Properly handled beaver castor can be purchased from most trapping supply firms; it is not cheap, but well worth the price.

The beaver is the second-largest rodent on earth, just behind the South American capybara. A male beaver can weigh as much as sixty pounds—sometimes bigger in extreme cases—and will live to about twenty-four years. The females can exceed the size of the males, a rare condition in most mammals. There are two species of beaver: the Eurasian beaver—*Castor fiber*—and the North American beaver—*Castor Canadensis*—though only the latter will concern us for the purposes of this book.

Beavers dwell in constructed lodges or houses as well as deep in the banks of streams and rivers. Beavers breed in the early part of the year and seem to mate for life. After a gestation period of about three months, two to six young are born on average. They depend on their mother's milk for at least the first month, when they can start to take in some solid food. By the time they are two months old they can survive on solid food entirely. The young can stay with their parents up to two years and are fully mature by the time they are three years old.

The beaver can remain underwater for up to fifteen minutes, which is handy for the construction and repair of their dams as well as for escaping predators. Their eyesight is poor, but their hearing, and senses of smell and touch, are very good. They are rather slow on land, but are fast swimmers. Beavers, like geese, will mate for life, but if one of the pair is killed or dies, the surviving beaver will pick another mate. Beavers are highly territorial, and as they are able to identify their family members from the scent produced by the anal glands (that puts a whole new spin on the family reunion), they will quickly confront another beaver from a different territory, resulting in a violent encounter. To avoid this, the beaver will use scent mounds or castor mounds to mark its territory quite often, and when approaching a beaver dam, you will probably be able to smell the beaver's marked mounds.

A beaver does the majority of its work in the dark. Dams will fail and need to be repaired, and the sound of rushing water—such as a break in a dam—will draw a beaver to that spot in the dam at dusk. A recording of rushing water has been used to draw a beaver out, for those who need to do control work to remove nuisance beavers. This diligent attention to repair is usually reserved for the primary dam system—beavers will build secondary and even tertiary dams on the watercourse—as this is what offers the necessary cover for the beaver's ecosystem. The secondary effects of the beaver's handiwork are both beneficial and destructive simultaneously. The artificial wetlands that the beaver creates becomes a home to many different species of wildfowl, yet the damming of a stream can affect those fish species that live in the faster flowing waters, as well as kill many different species of flora once the waters rise. "Beaver Fever" or Giardia—a parasite incorrectly attributed to the beaver ponds—has more to do with the parasitic infestation from feces-infested water than it does with beavers, but the connection will always be there.

The population of beavers across North America was estimated at over sixty million before the trapping boom of the seventeenth, eighteenth, and nineteenth centuries; today's estimates are between six and twelve million animals.

Traps

There are two main categories of traps for beaver, excluding snares: the leghold trap and the Conibear type (body-gripping traps). For the leghold type, both long spring and coil type are acceptable. Actually, the extra weight of the long-spring type can assist in the drowning of the animal. As for sizes, the leghold sizes I would recommend are No.3, No.4, and No.4½, coil spring or long spring. These traps should be equipped with extra-long strong chains. For the Conibear category, the No. 330 is the only one I would use, but some trappers have used the No.220 with some limited success. In my opinion, the No.330 Conibear is the most humane trap to use for beaver. When using the Conibear No. 330, especially for the first time, I recommend you purchase a pair of Conibear Setters; they come in different sizes. Purchase the largest ones, with the longest handles available. This larger

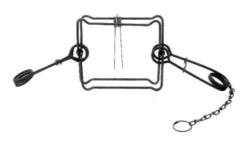

The perfect beaver trap, the #330 Conibear body-gripping trap.

size will give you the largest mechanical advantage, and will make setting the 330 Conibear much easier, especially when attempting to remove a large beaver from the trap. Also, you should always own and use a separate, unattached safety catch—designed just for the Conibear—and removing the safety catch should *always* be the last thing you do before you leave the set. These traps are very powerful, and are not to be taken lightly.

Lures

The lure most used in beaver trapping is beaver castor, as it is in my opinion the most effective lure you can use. There are some other types on the market, such as curiosity lures, but they are used much, much less than castor. As stated above, beaver are extremely territorial, and will investigate any scent (castor) of a strange beaver left behind in their domain. This is the main reason castor works so well.

Special Equipment

There are a few pieces of equipment that are almost a necessity when out to trap beaver. The first item is a good pair of insulated waders, as hip boots never seem to be high enough. Next is a pair of shoulder gauntlets; cold, wet arms make for a short day on a beaver trap line. Finally, if you are trapping a very large flooded swamp, lake, or large stream, you might consider a small johnboat or float that can be pulled behind you as you walk through the water. This is helpful when transporting your traps and equipment to your trap line and back, but is almost necessary when checking your traps. If you catch two or more fifty-plus-pound beavers—which is entirely possible—there is no way you can carry them and your equipment safely back to shore. Imagine being very far away from your mode of transportation, and having caught four, six, eight, or more beavers, plus your equipment; it is nearly impossible to deal with without some sort of means to safely transport them.

Sets

The following sets are for open-water conditions, or very light ice conditions. Trapping beaver under the thick ice and snow should only be attempted when you have a few years' experience under your belt or have a constant, well-experienced trapping partner who will be instructing you. Trapping beaver under the ice can be dangerous.

The Castor Mound Set

The castor mound set is a great set for beaver, as it can be constructed very quickly, used almost everywhere there are beaver, and is very productive. You can use either a leghold trap or Conibear. Both trap types will work well, it just depends where you pick your location for this set and the conditions already there, which will determine which type trap you utilize. Although you can always modify the natural conditions to your advantage, it is always best to capitalize on existing natural conditions.

Obviously, pick a spot where there is evidence of beavers traveling up and down the shoreline. Places where there are narrow canal-like entrances to the bank or a natural, small cove are ideal. The mound part of this set is usually basically constructed in same manner. It is made up of mud, grass, leaves, and twigs, taken out from the bottom of the stream, lake, or pond, right by the proposed set. Make a pile of this material about the size of a football about one to two feet off the shoreline. Place some beaver castor on top of the mound and cover it with a small piece of bark to keep it from drying out or being washed away by the rain. Now take your gloved hand and smear the bank about nine inches wide, right down to the shiny mud, from the mound to the water's edge, making it look like a freshly used, shiny slide. Use some branches and sticks on the back side of the mound to discourage the beaver from approaching the mound from any direction but from the water. If the water is at least a foot deep within three feet of the bank, I would use a No. 330 Conibear. If the water is not that deep, I would use a leghold trap. If using a Conibear, set it in water deep enough so the top of the trap will be about two inches below the water. I usually set the Conibear with the trigger and wires at the bottom; this will keep the chances of pelt damage to a minimum. Use two sticks, pushed into the mud, placed between the springs to hold the trap securely in place. These sticks should protrude out of the water. Tie off your trap to a stake, stationary object, or larger stick securely embedded in the mud. Next place a diving stick, about two to three inches in diameter and at least three feet long, horizontally directly over the trap, so it is touching the water. Secure this diving stick by either binding it into any vegetation on the sides of your approach or simply use two sticks at each end of the diving stick, also driven into the mud to keep it in place. A beaver swimming on the surface toward your set will naturally dive and swim just below the surface to avoid the "diving stick" and swim right through your trap. Use guide sticks, branches, or logs to guide the beaver in toward the shore and to your trap. In moderately populated areas, or in areas where there is any chance of domestic animals being in the area, like dogs and cats, I do not set a Conibear unless it can be totally submerged.

If the water is too shallow for a Conibear, or you only have a leghold trap available, we construct the trap site in the following manner: About one foot off the shore, offset three to four inches from being in line with your constructed slide, use your gloved hand to dig out a place for your trap. When set, the trap's pan should be six inches below the water, and placed so that the beaver will step between the jaws as opposed to over the jaws. You can improve your chances by placing an additional trap at least a foot farther out from the bank from and offset a few inches to the opposite side the first trap was offset. These traps should have long, strong chains, allowing the beaver to reach deep water and drown itself, if deeper water exists. Your trap should be secured to a stationary object or well-driven long stake.

The Run Set

Beavers use runs or roads in the water when traveling to and from their lodges, whether traveling to and from their feed piles or areas they are chewing down vegetation for building lodges, houses, or dams. If you walk in the water where these runs are, they sometimes have them worn down so that you can actually see the clean gravel bottom. There are places in deeper water where the vegetation has been worn away so it looks like a narrow channel or passageway through the cattails and such. Where these runs approach the shore, feed piles or their lodges makes great places for a set. I normally use No.330 Conibear for this set. If the water is not at the exact depth (too deep) so the trap can rest on the bottom, you simple wire your trap springs to two long poles and push the poles deep enough into the mud until the trap is a few inches under the water and secure. You can attach your dive stick to these poles as well. I recommend you attach your trap chain to a third well set stick off to the side. Again, I set the trap with the dog and trigger on the bottom.

The Leaky Dam Set

Beaver are always repairing leaks in their dams; this activity occupies most of their time. We can use this to our advantage, luring a beaver into a set. This set works best on secondary and even tertiary dams. Pick a spot on the dam, on the upstream side and as close to the dam as possible, but in deep enough water; set and conceal your Conibear trap wired on to two long poles. Push down the poles in the mud so that the set trap is just a few inches under the water. Place a dive stick across the top of your trap down to the top of the water.

Next, you'll need to make a small breach in the dam exactly opposite your trap. The leak should be large enough to be noticed by the beaver, but not so large as to lower the water level behind the dam. The beaver should swim straight to the leak, dive under your dive stick, and swim through your trap. You can place some branches on both sides of the trap to force the beaver into the path of your trap. *Author's Note*: Check the rules on trapping beaver in your area, as in some states it is not legal to set traps within a certain distance of a beaver dam.

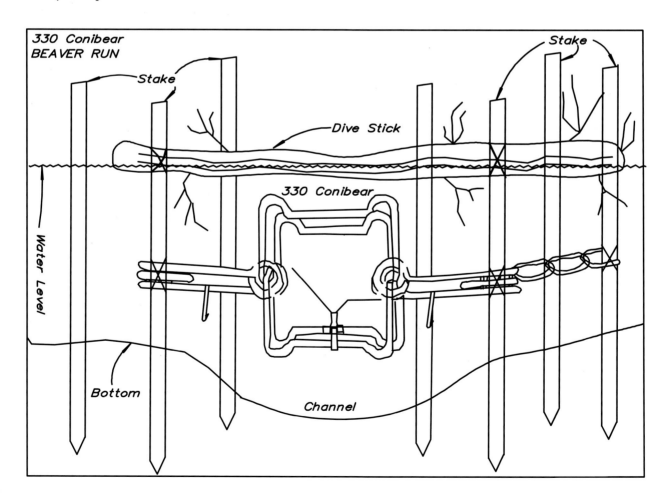

The Stick Set

In a spot with shallow water (four to six inches deep), and good beaver activity, drive a two-inch-diameter beaver-peeled stick in the mud, so it sticks out of the water about eighteen inches. About six inches out from the stick, set two leghold traps, each one on opposite sides of the stick, and anchor them well. On the top of the stick, place a good amount of a castor or curiosity lure, letting some run down the sides of the stick.

The Small Cove Set

Find a spot where the top of the bank is one foot high or less and the water is at least eighteen inches deep. While standing in the water, dig out a small cove about eighteen inches wide and two feet long, allowing it to flood with at least six inches of water. Place branches and debris around the three land sides of the cove, making sure the only clear approach is from the water. Just outside the entrance—about eighteen inches off shore—place your Conibear with two poles running through the springs holding it securely in place, so that the top of the trap is two inches below the water. Anchor this trap off. Now place your dive stick over your trap just touching the water. Next place additional guard sticks on the sides of the trap guarding the entrance so the only clear opening into the cove is by way of the trap.

You can bait the cove in two ways. One is to place some fresh poplar or willow sticks in the cove by pushing them into the mud a short distance, leaving them slicking out of the water at least eighteen inches or more. The other method of baiting is to drive a stick in the center of the cove and place a piece of beaver castor on the top of the stick. If you are not able to use a Conibear, you can use a leghold trap with a long chain bedded in the six-inch-deep portion of the cove. Anchor the leghold trap to something secure.

The Feeder Stream Set

In a narrow, deep feeder stream, which can be as little as one to two feet wide, place a dive stick or log that is at least four inches in diameter across the entire feeder stream, with the entire bottom of the dive stick touching the water. In the center of the feeder steam, right under the dive stick, place your Conibear, with the trigger and dog on the bottom, using sticks to hold it in place so that the top of the trap is just below the water. Secure your trap off to the side of the feeder stream. Next set a few vertical sticks on the mud on both sides of the trap. The only clear opening under the dive stick should be your trap. Beavers are constantly exploring these small feeder streams, and this set will get them.

The Dam Slide or Crossover Set

On every beaver dam, there is a spot or two where beavers routinely cross over the dam for one reason or another. They seem to use the same spot over and over, creating a slide; these slides are called crossovers, and they are one of the best places to make a leghold trap set. I have noticed that this set works best for me on secondary and even tertiary dams. Once you find one of these crossover slides, study it very carefully, looking at both ends of the slide. When you do, you will see the spot where the beaver places his feet just before using the slide to go over the dam and where the beaver places its feet as he exits the slide at the bottom. These spots are where you place your leghold traps. There should be a few inches of water at these locations. When making this set, you should be standing in the water if at all possible.

When setting at the top of the slide, anchor your trap on the back side of the dam with a long chain. Camouflage the trap with mud from the base of the dam. The trap pan should be within three to four inches below the water if possible. If setting on the downstream end of the slide or crossover, the trap should be set in the same manner, but tied off or staked to the side. At this set, I have used a little beaver castor on a stick or rock just upstream and to the side of the slide and the trap. This set at the bottom of the slide is usually far enough away from the dam to be legal, if there are restrictions on setting traps on beaver dams.

Again: Check the rules on trapping beavers in your area, as in some states it is not legal to set traps within a certain distance of a beaver dam.

Once you've successfully trapped your beaver, remember that beavers are open skinned as opposed to cased. Please see the chapter on skinning, fleshing, and stretching in Part Five of this book. Beaver, badgers, wolverines, and bears are the only animals that I know of that are skinned open; all other animals are cased.

Otter — The River Predator

The North American river otter is a semi-aquatic furbearing mammal that is found along the numerous waterways and wetlands of the East and West coasts of the United States, in the area surrounding the Great Lakes and Mississippi River basin, the wet Pacific Northwest, and the greater portion of Canada.

The river otter's sleek body design, not to mention a set of sharp teeth, makes it an efficient predator in the water. It will feed on fish, crustaceans, insects, small birds, and small reptiles. They favor slow-moving water, and will often share the same habitat as beavers, enjoying freshwater marshlands, boggy lakes, and so on.

The river otter will weigh between ten and thirty pounds—the males are considerably larger than the females—and have a body length of twenty-six to forty-two inches, with an additional twelve- to twenty-inch-long tail. Their thick, brown fur is water-repellent, and has been prized by trappers for centuries. The otter is a muscular animal, with a thick neck the same diameter as its head, short limbs, small ears, and mouthful of large teeth. They are classified as *Lontra canadensis*, being distantly related to the weasel family.

Otters will live for up to ten years in the wild, and females will begin breeding at two years of age.

The otter, predator of the rivers. (Photo Credit: Getty Images.)

With a sleek body design and sharp canine teeth, the otter makes an efficient predator. (Photo Credit: Getty Images.)

They mate between December and April—sometimes in the water, and sometimes on land—yet, like the fisher, the otter has a delayed gestation. The fertilized eggs go dormant for eight months, but begin development the following winter, and after a gestation period of sixty-two days the mother will give birth to one to three pups. The females will choose a den site borrowed from another animal—usually a beaver, fox, or woodchuck—and will raise their young on their own, keeping the offspring with them for a year.

An otter is equally at home on the land or water, and can cover the real estate rather quickly in either situation. They are naturally inquisitive, and a trapper can use that to his advantage. Since the otter will share turf with a beaver, the two are often targeted by a trapper at the same time. They are sensitive to environmental changes, like the wetlands and watercourses themselves, and otter populations have been compromised by settlement and sprawl. They are social animals, with males forming bachelor groups, and the females staying with their young for the first year; you will often find the animals in groups while scouting for them.

This stream is a perfect place for otter trapping.

Traps

Otters are large and very strong. I would recommend a No.3 or even a No.4 leghold trap for otters. The No. 4½ would not be too large, depending on the set. Coil spring or long spring type are both satisfactory. As for body-gripping traps, I would stick with a No. 330. Otters travel in the same waters that beavers do, so the No.330 will still take a beaver that happens into an otter set.

Otter tracks.

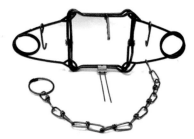

The #330 Conibear makes an excellent trap for otters.

Lures and Bait

The most effective lure for otter is otter musk; next down the list would be beaver castor. Mink gland lure will also bring in any otter. Otters will kill every mink they can catch, as they are natural enemies. Any set that smells like a mink will cause an otter to investigate thoroughly. As for bait, otters are strictly meat eaters, with fish being their favorite meal, especially trout; frogs and crayfish are also a favorite. They have been known to kill and eat muskrats as well. Trappers often use beaver flesh and muskrat flesh in their baited sets as a meat-based lure.

Special Equipment

Otters are always near water, although they come out of the water much more often than beaver will. They use streams like we would use a trail to get from one place to another. Hip boots are must and waders—though a bit more cumbersome—would be completely appropriate. They use slides like beavers when coming out of or going into the water. With few exceptions, all sets for otters should be water sets, and set up for a drown set whenever possible, especially when using leghold traps. Longer trap chains

and a spool of heavy gauge wire should definitely be added to your trap basket.

Sets

The Beaver Dam Set

Otters hang around beaver dams, probably because there are usually minnows trapped once the dam is constructed, making for easy meals. If the dam is abandoned, you can open up a channel, allowing the water to flow. Otters will use the constructed channel to exit the large pond area behind the dam. You should carefully conceal a trap in the channel, right where the water is going over the dam, in the same manner that the beaver set is made in a dam breach. This set should be set up for a drown set or a body-gripping trap.

The Mink Post

In water at least two feet deep, and as close to the middle of a stream as possible, sink a three-inch-diameter post or log, so it sticks out of the water about eighteen inches. Next pile rocks around the entire base of the post, until there is a flat area of rock to set your leghold traps on, four to six inches below the water. Set a trap on both the upstream and downstream side of the post and tie off your traps to deeper water. On one side of the post, place some otter musk (as a gland lure) and on the other side place a good mink gland lure.

Small Stream Channel Set

In a small feeder stream, you can close up the stream channel, leaving only a one-foot-wide channel or small spillway. You can easily conceal your trap in this channel. You can use a body-gripping trap or leghold. Both should be camouflaged well and be odorless.

Toilet Set

Otters create and use certain spots for toilets. Each spot is made up of otter scat, vomit, fish bones, fish scales, and the like. These toilets are usually very close the water. If you find one, study it closely, and see where the otter enters and exits the body of water to visit the toilet. Set a trap in two to three inches of water at the spot where they enter and exit; tie it off to deep water to drown the catch. Camouflage the trap as well as you can. Otters usually travel in pairs, so it would behoove you to make another set nearby.

Fish Set

You'll want to use a No. 330 body-gripping trap for this set. Securely wire the trap to a pole. Place a dead fish (or fake one if you cannot get a real one) on one of the trigger wires. Make sure it is affixed well enough so it will not come off. Now place the pole into a stream bed, so the fish is about one foot under the water. Make sure the pole is steady; you may have to attach it to an overhanging limb or add a cross pole to steady it. Tie off the trap to a stationary object. Turn the trap so the fish is pointing upstream. You can place some otter musk on the pole, about one foot above the water, to act as an attractant.

Special Note: Otter fur—whether the otter is alive or dead—will "singe" if out of the water and exposed to the sun for any length of time. This is where the ends of each individual hair will curl at the end, instead of remaining straight. To avoid this, you

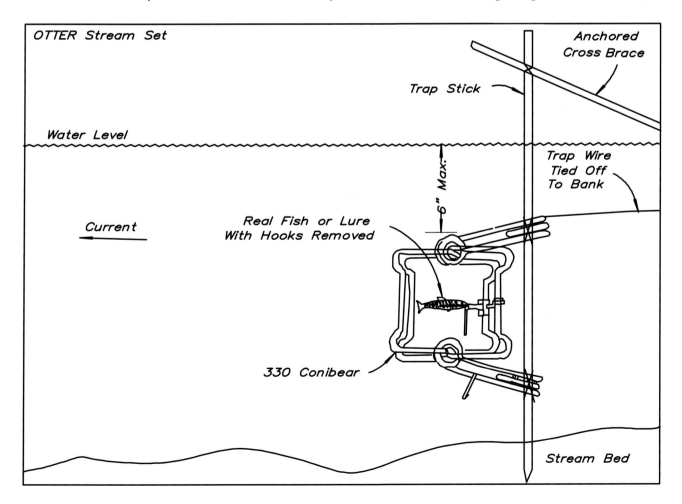

A brace of stinkers. (Photo Credit: Getty Images.)

should place the wet otter in a wet bag, if you don't plan to get it home to skin directly.

The Skunk—Smelly and Striped!

The famous black and white skunk—well-armed with a defense mechanism that will make predators run—populates nearly all of the continental United States, southern Canada, and northern Mexico. He is recognizable at a glance, though the classic striped skunk—*mephitis mephitis*—is not the only species to inhabit our continent. As a matter of fact, Texas alone has five different species of skunks, all with different fur markings. All species of skunks come with their own set of issues, namely the smell. Their fur is very attractive and luxurious, however, and it was the target of trappers during the era of exploration, being one of the most popular species taken at that time, behind beaver and muskrat. A prime skunk pelt makes a unique and attractive hat.

Skunks have short legs, standing low to the ground, and will measure between sixteen and thirty-eight inches, weighing from one to eighteen pounds, depending on the species and location. A skunk has long front claws, perfect for digging; in your travels in the wilderness you will find where skunks may have dug out a bee's nest for the grubs, or you may find holes dug in your lawn where a skunk has searched for grubs and worms. Their fur is black, with some sort of contrasting white stripes (or spots in some species), and has a deep shine to it. The white markings can range from snow white to a cream color. The male skunks are a bit larger than the females, and they will pair up to mate in the early spring. During the winter months skunks will seek a den, though they will not hibernate, with males remaining solitary and females gathering together in groups of up to a dozen. After a gestation period of sixty-six days, the females will give birth to four to seven young, called kits, in a den she has prepared for them. The kits' eyes open at about three weeks of age, and mother will wean them at two to three months. Mother raises the young alone, and they will stay with her for about a year.

A skunk on the prowl. (Photo Credit: Getty Images.)

The skunk is an omnivore—and quite the scavenger at that—that will take advantage of a multitude of opportunities. Bird's nests, dumpsters, and garbage cans are all fair game; in the wild the skunk will eat insects, eggs, chicks, small rodents, shellfish, berries, and corn. The skunk does whatever it must to survive. They are crepuscular, meaning they are primarily nocturnal, but will be active during the hours just before dusk and just after dawn.

The skunk's main form of defense is the horrible smelling liquid they spray; it is contained in two glands, one on each side of the anus. When threatened, the skunk will raise its tail, in an aggressive posture, and when it has had enough will turn its rump at the enemy and use the pair of glands immediately on either side of the anus to accurately disperse a healthy dose of what may be the most pungent and foul-smelling solution in the natural world, called skunk essence, up to ten feet in distance. This skunk essence can cause permanent blindness in dogs and humans. Humans can detect the smell of this solution at a distance of over three miles. Skunk essence is harvested by trappers and used in lure making. Good and well-handled skunk essence is selling for about twenty dollars per ounce. In this chapter, I will give you a method of harvesting skunk essence from a skunk without having to skin the skunk first. Not only is this method less messy, but it makes skinning the skunk afterwards much less of a smelly job.

Skunks are the prey of a number of different species—though only in times of duress, as the skunk's defense system is that effective—including bobcats, coyotes, mountain lions, and foxes, as well as the larger birds of prey, especially the great horned owl. Skunks are also a huge carrier and transmitter of rabies, almost as much as the raccoon. Because

Classic skunk pose, on the prowl for an opportunity.

of their defensive mechanism, most animals—and humans—leave them alone, so they can become rather prolific breeders. Some of our local villages here in the Hudson Valley have been inundated with skunks; nightly sightings are a common occurrence, and skunk/pet conflicts are equally common. Trapping them is a highly effective tool to control their numbers. Skunks are regularly taken as non-target animals in predator sets.

Traps

Skunks can be readily taken in most any type trap, except the "dog-proof coon trap." Leghold, body-gripping, and live cage traps are all perfect choices for skunk trapping. The size of the leghold traps I use for skunk is mainly No. 1½ or No. 2.; whether double coil or long spring really does not make much of a difference. If you have any double-jaw traps in the sizes mentioned above, I would advise using them to prevent any chew offs. As for body-gripping traps, the No.120 Conibear is my trap of choice. The No. 110 will work fine, but I prefer the No. 120, mainly because it will hold and kill a raccoon that might wander into my skunk set. Live, cage-type traps are fine, as skunks have no fear of walking right into them. I always use a little larger size live trap than necessary, say at least 12x14x36-inch, again for the simple reason that you never know when Mr. Ringtail might get there before your intended skunk.

Also, I like the style of live trap that opens at both

Skunk tracks in the mud.

ends when set, as opposed the style that only opens at one end. Most animals will more freely go into a cage trap if they can see right through it. These cage traps are ideal when trapping skunks around houses and barns. The major advantage with the use of cage traps in these areas, is that you are always able release a non-target catch such as the neighbor's cat or small dog unharmed. Always tie down your cage trap to something stationary, if at all possible, when you place them. This prevents the chances of a cage roll-over, which might allow the caged animal to escape.

Lures

There are several commercial skunk lures offered for sale on the market today. Most are food lures, but there are some specifically intended for cage traps and some are mating scent lures.

Bait

Bait for skunk is relatively easy to obtain from home. Some possibilities are raw fish, bacon drippings, chicken entrails and parts (with the feathers on or off), and loud cheeses, such as limburger or gorgonzola.

Sets

The Cross Log Set

This set can be constructed and pre-baited long (two to four weeks) before trapping season. This will get the animals used coming to the set without any fear. Also, when the season opens you just have to set your traps, bait the hole, and you are on your way. Take four logs of four to six inches in diameter, about four feet in length or longer. Arrange them on a clear, level surface in the form of a large X or cross. Pull each log back about six inches from where they would normally intersect, creating a gap in the center of the X or cross about one foot square. Use four short wood stakes, two at each end and on both sides of each log, to secure it. In the center of this gap, dig a shallow hole about six inches in diameter and six inches deep, as this will act as your bait hole. Place about two

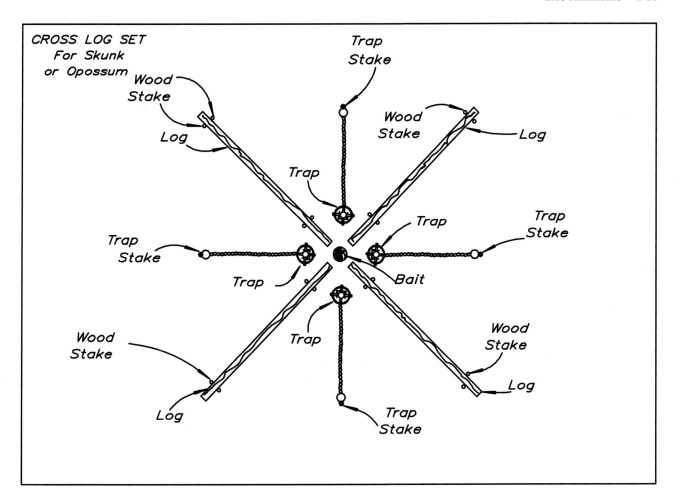

CROSS LOG SET
For Skunk
or Opossum

inches of dry grass in the bottom of the bait hole, and put your bait of choice on top of the dry grass. Put enough bait to fill the hole within two inches of the top. Now cover the bait with more dry grass and cover it with a large piece of bark. This will keep crows and other birds from scavenging the bait. Next, about one foot back from the edge of the bait hole, and between a set of logs, set a trap just below ground level with a pan cover, and lightly cover the trap with sifted dirt. Set your trap stake in the opposite direction from the bait hole, as far as the trap chain allows. Do this in all four quadrants of the X. You can add a few small, stepping guide sticks to the sets. When you are done, you will have one bait hole and four set traps. This set has really produced for me, with as many as three catches in one night. This set also works well for raccoons and opossum. The attached diagram should explain and help you understand what I have just described.

The Dirt Hole Set

The dirt hole set as described in the fox and coyote chapters will also take a skunk. Use a No.2 trap, and prepare the set as if you were setting it for a fox. Use a loud skunk bait or skunk lure at this set. In addition to a good skunk lure, I use over-fried chicken skin and over-fried bacon or ham trimmings for bait. I have caught many gray foxes when setting for skunk with the dirt hole set. When setting for skunk at a dirt hole, set use a large drag or a grapple instead of staking the trap to the set. This makes resetting the set much easier, and saves you precious time.

The Cubby Set

The cubby set for skunks is very productive, and will work in most all types of weather. When constructing a cubby for skunks, I make them a little larger than cubbys intended for other furbearers. I construct the cubby at least a month before its intended use. This allows me to do all the time-consuming work, which will require carrying some tools, in better weather and then start pre-season baiting. The size of the cubby for skunk that I try to achieve is a cubby that is about two feet wide, eighteen inches high, and three feet long. It can be made out of logs, sticks, stones, or a combination of all three. It should have a roof or cover to keep out the elements, but the cubby must have only one entrance. You can place pine branches, brush, or leaves over it after it is built to hide the set from passersby and scavenging birds. Again, I use a very loud bait when pre-baiting at first; after you have the animals coming on a regular basis, you can use most anything. When the season opens, and the fur is prime, you want to start trapping this cubby. Set two traps at the entrance, or one trap right at the entrance and one a foot or so back out from the first trap. I would use a No. 1½ or No. 2 at the cubby, tie the traps off to a large drag, or if choosing to stake your traps, then place the stake as far away from the cubby entrance as possible. If you wish to use a Conibear-style trap, use a No. 120. To utilize this style trap, you must restrict the size of the opening to just fit the size of the trap, about a seven-inch square opening. You can also make two separate seven-inch square openings and deploy two traps. Stake down or tie off these traps to a stationary object, as this not only prevents the animal from getting away from a poor grip, but prevents the dead animal in your trap from being carried off by a larger non-trapped animal which happens along.

Ground Bee Sets

Skunks routinely dig out bees' nests located in the ground or stumps, in order to feed on them. In my travels over the years, I have noticed hundreds of yellow jacket nests that have been ravaged by skunks. The skunks do this at night, when the bees are much less able to sting the skunk to drive it off. As far as I am concerned, the more yellow jacket nests they devour, the better, as there are few summers that go by when I don't end up stepping on or just disturbing one of these nests, and end up getting stung multiple times. I have also noticed that after the skunk has completely cleaned out the nest, they return days

later to the same nest to look for more bees. This is a trait we trappers can use to our advantage. If you find one of these nests that have been destroyed by a skunk, the first thing to do is stand back a few feet and observe if there are any surviving bees around or going in and out of the torn up bees' nest. I have seen, several times, a nest that looks on the surface to have been totally destroyed and abandoned, but on closer inspection there were a few bees still living there. These survivors will sting you!

If the nest looks completely empty, take a stick and poke and prod around to make totally sure. If this site is free of bees, you are now able to make your set. About six inches out from the edge of the skunk's excavation, using your hand, smooth and level out a spot a little larger than your trap. Remove any stones or debris and set them to the side. Next dig out a shallow trap bed, and bed and stake your trap. I would use a size No. 1½ or No. 2, with a double jaw, if you have any. Place a pan cover over the pan and tuck it under the loose jaw. Make sure there is a tear in the pan cover right over the dog of the trap. Position the trap for a step between the jaw catch and so the pan is about six inches out from the edge of the excavation. Now cover the trap with sifted excavated material. Next, using the small stones and sticks you removed, make a small one-half-inch-high by one-inch-wide berm, in a semi-circle around the outside half of the concealed trap, about one inch out from the body of the trap, to act as a stepping device. Last thing is to place a few drops of a skunk lure on the top edge of the skunk's excavation and in the excavation itself.

Skunk Essence Harvesting

Skunk essence is the obnoxious smelling liquid that the skunk disperses when implementing its defense mechanism. It is very strong and almost burns the senses. When it comes in contact with the eyes of a human or dog, it has been known to cause permanent blindness. The best household remedy that is most used to remove the smelly stuff is tomato juice. The part of the essence that makes it smell and burn so badly is called *sulphide mercaptan*. The two sacks that accurately dispense this liquid are located right next to and on each side of the skunk's anus. There is one nipple protruding out of each sack that can be fired separately or both simultaneously. Skunk essence is used as an additive in the production of great many trapping lures, for a vast variety of different furbearers. It is also just used straight, just how nature made it, for attracting animals.

Good skunk essence sells for about twenty dollars per ounce. It will eat right through plastic and metal containers, and should only be stored in clean, glass containers. For smaller amounts use "Boston Round Glass Bottles," but make sure you get the type that come with heavy, hard, black plastic caps, and not metal caps. Over time the essence eats through the thin metal caps and exposure to the air will spoil the essence. For larger amounts you can use an old wine or whiskey bottle with hard plastic cap. I never fill any container/bottle up to the very top with essence.

The first thing to do is pick a stable spot (you most definitely want to be outdoors, away from your house) to work on, like an old table, covered with a piece of plastic. If there is any moving air, you want the wind to be at your back. To extract the essence, place the skunk on its back so you can lean it a little to one side or the other. Wearing a pair of surgical gloves, gently feel around and locate the exact location of the sack you wish to extract the essence from. Using a high-capacity syringe with an 18-gauge needle, gently push the needle right through the center of the sack. While pulling back on the syringe plunger, applying vacuum, pull the needle back slowly until you see the reddish essence filling the syringe. Keeping the needle at that location in the sack and, still applying vacuum, gently wiggle the needle until no more essence comes out of the sack. Stop applying vacuum and remove the syringe, and when the needle is completely out of the skunk, tip the needle upward. Now empty the contents in the syringe into your Boston Round Glass Bottle. You can repeat the retrieval process on the same sack to ensure you have harvested all the essence in that sack. Take special care not to pull the plunger all the way out the back of the syringe, as this will be an

unforgettable experience. Now repeat the whole process on the other sack. Cover the bottle tightly when done. Once the harvesting has been completed properly, the skunk is now safe and much more pleasant to skin. At times, one sack will be almost empty and the other totally full.

When you are finished with harvesting the essence, stick the needle in a bowl or jar of water and completely rinse the inside of the syringe by pulling the plunger back and forth several times, making sure the whole length of the inside of the syringe has been rinsed. Expel any water left in the syringe. If you fail to do this every time you extract essence, the residue will corrode and melt the syringe and render it useless. After letting the extracted essence set still for a day or so, you will notice that there is cloudy sediment at the bottom of the bottle. This is called the "mustard." Carefully and slowly pour off the top fluid into a clean, larger vessel, leaving the mustard behind. You now have "Pure Skunk Essence" that can be used for a home-made trapping lure, or sold for profit.

The Opossum—the North American marsupial

Playing 'possum.

In our slang, it means to pretend to be dead, based on the defense mechanism of the opossum. When threatened or stressed, North America's only marsupial—*didelphis virginiana*—will most certainly lie down and pretend to have passed onto the next life. The opossum—unlike most of our North American fauna—actually migrated northerly from South America. It inhabits a good part of the eastern United States, from the East Coast to the Mississippi River, northerly to the Canadian border, as well as having a healthy population on the West Coast.

The opossum is a nocturnal animal, quite comfortable living near human habitation and rather fond of the food sources humans create. They will revel in rooting through garbage cans and dumpsters alike, raid henhouses for eggs, and participate

North America's only marsupial, the opossum. (Photo Credit: Getty Images.)

in any other scavenger activities that will provide food. In the wild, the opossum acts like a vacuum cleaner, eating fruits, grains, insects, slugs, frogs, salamanders, rodents, carrion, and just about anything else it can digest. Being nocturnal, the opossum will spend the daytime hours in a 'day den,' such as a hollow log or tree. Recent studies have shown that the opossum is nearly immune to Lyme disease, and will actually consume up to 96 percent of the ticks on their bodies, with no ill effect. Compare that to the mice and shrews that harbor and spread the Lyme tick, and you may see the opossum in a different light. The immune system of the opossum is so well constructed that it it also apparently immune to the effects of snake venom.

The opossum is about the same size as a large house cat, yet has several physical features that are interesting and unique. The opossum's prehensile tail can be used to grab branches, and even to hang from. The tail, like the ears, is hairless, and the white, elongated rat-like face ends in a pink nose. The opossum's long jaws contain a total of fifty teeth, and the females carry thirteen nipples: twelve in a circular pattern and one in the center.

The size and weight of an opossum can vary greatly, depending on the climate in which it lives. The northern climes will see animals considerably larger than the southern areas, with the smallest females weighing in at about one pound and the largest males weighing as much as fourteen or fifteen pounds. They have a hand-like footprint, with the rear foot featuring a splayed thumb; this will be clearly evident when you see an opossum's tracks in the mud.

Opossum will have up three litters per year, after a gestation period of thirteen days, of up to twenty

Tracks of the opossum in the snow.

(and sometimes as many as thirty) joeys per litter, yet due to the amount of nipples, only thirteen will survive. They spend the first couple of months in their mother's pouch, and then the opossum will carry its young on its back. The opossum has a relatively short lifespan, usually of just two years, yet sometimes as long as four years under optimum conditions.

The opossum is taken in high numbers each year for its fur, as it makes for attractive clothing and blankets. Many opossums are taken incidentally at raccoon, skunk, fox, and coyote sets. Opossums are a little more difficult to kill, so make sure they are dead before attempting to remove them from any trap.

Traps

Any trap advocated in the chapter on skunk will work equally as well for opossum. One thing to keep in mind is that opossums can and will readily climb trees, as skunks do not. So if you used a too light a

A mother opossum carrying her young. (Photo Credit: Getty Images.)

The opossum can easily climb trees. (Photo Credit: Getty Images.)

drag, or for some reason your stake was pulled out, when looking for the opossum, look up into the trees.

Bait

Any bait used for skunk or foxes will work for opossum. I have caught too many opossums in my fox sets unintentionally.

Lure

There are some lures on the market that state they are for opossum. I think most of them are the same as for skunk but with different labels. Most lures sold and used for opossum are accurately labeled "Skunk and Opossum." This should tell you something.

Sets

All sets that are mentioned in the chapter on skunks are just as effective on opossum. In fact, opossums are really easier to set for, as they will walk right into a bare, uncovered trap. I would still camouflage any set intended for opossum, because you never know when a smarter furbearer will investigate your set. The Cubby and Cross Log sets have worked the best for me.

Ermine — A Weasel in the White

The tiny weasel, or stoat, makes an amazing transformation in the winter, where its brown fur coat turns a frosty white, and it becomes known as

Brown in the summer and white in the winter; the weasel/ermine.

A weasel, taken during a henhouse raid, still in summer coat.

ermine. Though tiny, ermine are ferocious predators. The ermine population runs from the northern border states of the US up into the higher latitudes of Canada and Alaska. A weasel is wily, intelligent, and inventive; if you've ever had a weasel invade a henhouse, you know just how crafty they can be, squeezing through the tiniest of crevices in order to feast.

The ermine's body will measure between six and twelve inches in length; males will weigh around nine ounces, with females weighing six. In opposition to Bergmann's Rule—where animals at the higher latitudes tend to increase in size—the ermine will get smaller the further north you go. Their bodies are low to the ground, with short limbs, and an ermine will investigate the smallest nooks and crannies; as trappers, we can use that to our advantage, as my pal Matthew Breuer is about to demonstrate.

One of Breuer's catches in his ermine box.

Building the Box—by Matthew Breuer

Everyone has some spare lumber lying around, and the best way to trick the kings of trickery is with weasel boxes. It just requires a quick trip to the shop to pick out some boards, measure them, and cut them to size, and you are off and running. The dimensions for weasel boxes include a front and rear measuring six and three-eighths inches long, sides measuring twelve inches long, a bottom measuring twelve inches long, and a top measuring eighteen inches long. The top of the box should have an overhang to keep out snow, and it's a great place to grab the trap when carrying it or placing it. All of the boards are roughly five and one-half inches wide, giving the traps we utilize the perfect fit. Using one and one-half-inch No. 6 sheetrock screws, assemble the box, leaving the top piece unattached. Next, using a two-inch wood hole bit, drill a hole in the front of the box, slightly above center. This makes the ermine have to climb up into the box, even if there's a bit of snow.

Another victim of the ermine box.

Using a one-half-inch wood hole bit, cut several holes in the back of the box, which will allow for scent to disperse from the box. The last steps are to drill two holes in the back of the box, and the top of the box. Then, using trapping wire, thread it through those holes, attaching the top and back, utilizing the wire as a hinge. Use two more screws, partially screwed into each side. Again, using trapping wire, run a long piece from one screw to the other, leaving some leftover to wrap around one side. This will act as a "lock" to keep the top closed, and keep critters like raccoons from stealing your bait. Attach your trap tag with a screw to the top of the box, and you're all set.

The entrance hole of the ermine box.

Traps and Bait

Some people like #1 long springs in their boxes. I prefer Victor rat traps with the large cheese pan, as they are plenty strong, and provide a large stepping pad for the ermine to set off the trap. They also fit perfectly inside of the custom boxes. The weasel has to go over the trap on the way in or out.

The inside of the ermine box, with rat trap.

Baits vary, and to be honest, whatever you have for meat will likely work. I've used everything from deer fat and scraps, beaver meat, to chicken liver. Lure is optional. Typically unfrozen bloody meat is more than enough to lure in the small but ferocious predators. Simply put a cut of meat in the back of the box, with the trap in the front, near the entrance hole.

Locations

Ermine love swampy areas with a lot of small hiding places. Fields, clear-cuts, cedar swamps, marshes, and beaver pond edges are all great options. If your state allows trapping in culverts, utilize them. Weasels love traveling through them chasing rabbits or moving from one area to another without having to cross a road. They also work as a pinch point, forcing the weasels to get close to your set. Simply set the box on the outer edge of the culvert. Be sure it's not sitting in any water, as you can ruin the box, and you run the risk of it freezing in.

Ermine tracks in the snow.

Market Value

There are a few types of ermine; least weasel, short-tailed weasel, and long-tailed weasels are the most common. Here in northern Minnesota, we're after short-tailed weasels, as the other species are rare. All species of ermine change colors to adapt to the weather. In the spring and summer they are brown, with some white on their bellies, and the signature black tip on the tail. In late fall they begin to turn white, and by Christmas they are as white as snow. This is when their fur is prime.

Skinning and stretching ermine is very simple, but can be tedious due to their small size. Skinning them while they are warm is easiest, and building your own stretchers is recommended. A simple cut of wood and some sanding, and you're in business. Inside out with the tail stripped is the method. A prime ermine will bring anywhere from one to twelve dollars in the current market. Ten to twelve dollars would be a top lot, prime buck ermine. Expect an average of two to four dollars per ermine. As with muskrats, weasel trapping is a numbers game. Putting out thirty weasel boxes can more than pay for your gas money along the line on a good day.

Part 5

Tips of The Trade

Dispatching a Trapped Animal—Tools and Techniques

Congratulations, everything went according to plan, and you've been rewarded for your hard work by seeing the animal you are after firmly held in your trap. Before you can begin the skinning and stretching processes, you must first dispatch the animal, as humanely as possible. There are several means of accomplishing the task, and I want to reinforce the fact that no matter what may make perfect sense, always make sure your actions are within the boundaries of the local law covering the area in which you are trapping. I will state the obvious: A drown set for beaver, muskrat, mink, otter, or raccoon will avoid the need to dispatch the animal, as it should be deceased when you check the trap. Land sets, however, require you to kill the animal. Let's look at some of the tools and methods available.

Firearms

A firearm is the best tool for neatly dispatching a furbearer, and there are many affordable options that will handle the job. Portability is going to be the key here, as you'll have a basket full of tools to begin with, and the shot distances are going to be very short. Regarding caliber, I would say the .22 rimfire cartridges are the handiest, are readily available, and offer the best balance of portability/affordability/effectiveness. Quite obviously, the .22 Long Rifle cartridge has been—and will continue to be—the most popular of the lot. If you tailor your firearm choice, you may also use the .22 Long and .22 Short ammunition in a .22 Long Rifle chamber. The use of the less powerful ammunition minimizes pelt damage, as well as reducing the report of the firearm—drawing less attention to your activities.

There are many reliable rimfire rifles, and your trapping gun certainly doesn't need to be high-tech; an old single shot will work just fine, as will a small lever action. The goal here is just to have a gun that will go bang every time. No scope will be needed—iron sights are just fine—nor will a magazine, as one shot at close range will most often suffice.

The highly popular Henry Rimfire lever–action rimfire has sold over 1,000,000 units.

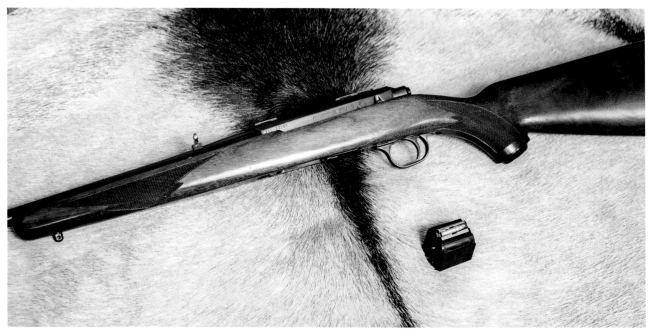

Philip P. Massaro's Ruger Model 77/22, a longtime friend and good choice for a trapline.

The Henry Classic Lever Action .22 comes quickly to mind, as its lightweight design and affordable price are perfect for a rifle that will see the day-to-day chores of the trapper, without breaking the bank. Though it has a tubular magazine, the .22 Short ammunition can easily be fed directly into the chamber, and the rifle can fill other roles, such as target shooting and plinking, or those fun autumn squirrel hunts. If you nose around the gun shops, there are plenty of good deals on used Remington, Winchester, Marlin, and Stevens rifles.

The bottom line is that I wouldn't take a prized .22 rimfire with me to check my trap line; I'd rather find a functional "beater" that will take the punishment of the trapping season without marring and scarring a prized or collectable firearm. Trapping and

My early 1970s Ruger Single Six, in .22 Long Rifle.

inclement weather go hand-in-hand (traps *must* be checked every day, not just in fair weather), so if you find a model with a synthetic stock and stainless-steel finish, all the better. I would, however, do a bit of practicing with the rifle, as I've had an animal pull out of a trap and try to run away as I approached the set; I've been able to shoot them at thirty to forty yards as they tried to escape.

A handgun is a more efficient tool to carry for the dispatch of a furbearer, as it can be worn in a holster on your hip, leaving your hands (and shoulder) free from encumbrance.

For years I have carried a Ruger Single Six six-shot revolver. The grips are nearly devoid of finish, and the bluing is nearly gone for the first one and one-half inches of the barrel, but if I could tally the amount of animals that pistol has taken—between trapping and those years I ran 'coon hounds—I bet you'd be astonished. The single-action revolver is one of the simplest designs, making it one of the safest as well. It can be operated with gloved hands, and must be deliberately worked in order to go off. The Ruger Single Six is just one example of a rimfire revolver—there are many new and old designs that make an excellent choice—but that design has worked well for me since the early 1970s.

Air Guns

As silly as it may sound, the modern high-powered air gun makes a solid choice for the trapper, and especially for those trappers who have taken their safety course and are old enough to have a license, but are too young to carry a firearm in the field. Modern .22- and .25-caliber air rifles from companies like Crosman and Benjamin can easily mimic the performance of the .22 Short (which uses a 29-grain bullet at just about 1,100 fps) without the noise associated with a firearm. Is an air gun going to be everyone's cup of tea? Probably not, but in the suburban areas—where the report of a supersonic cartridge will certainly result in a call to the authorities—an air gun makes an awful lot of sense, and it probably wouldn't be a bad idea to add one to your collection.

Alternative Means

I knew older trappers who never took a gun of any sort with them in order to check their trap line. In

Whoa Dad, not me!

order to dispatch an animal, they would use a club—in this instance a bat made from a piece of hickory, about two feet long—and would strike the trapped animal on the head twice; the first time to stun the animal and render it unconscious, the second to crush the skull and deliver the killing blow.

You can ensure the animal is dead by using a stick to touch its eyeball; all animals, regardless of how wounded they may be, will involuntarily blink when the eyeball is touched. Of all the animals to be trapped, the opossum may be the most difficult to kill; they are just naturally tough. If not using a firearm, place a stout stick across the opossum's neck, stand on either end of the stick to pin it down, and pull up violently on the tail, thereby breaking the animal's neck.

Many objects can be used to crush an animal's skull, such as an ax handle, heavy dead branch, or any other improvised club, and the old-timers preferred this as it produced the least amount of blood at the trap set. This method of dispatching an animal was also part of the New York State Trapper's Education curriculum at least until the early 1980s. While today's politically correct activists would probably faint at the concept, the stark fact is that the animal is going to die, and while we need not revel in the act of killing, we shouldn't shy away from the fact that it must be done to control populations.

Though I wouldn't condemn anyone for using the above described methods, I personally prefer to use either a firearm or air gun, as I feel it is the most efficient and humane method of dispatching an animal.

Skinning, Stretching, and Fleshing

You've worked very hard to scout your area, tune your traps and keep your equipment in top shape, make your sets just so, and score on an animal with prime fur. It's now time to discuss how to handle the fur, including the proper skinning, stretching, and fleshing of the hide.

The first thing you'll have to do is skin the animal, and that might not be so easy until you become experienced at it. So, I would advise that you practice on some animals with "inexpensive" fur. Woodchucks in the summer are often taken as garden pests, and are absolutely perfect to practice on. Additionally, squirrels, rabbits, and other small animals can be used for practice—when in season—or road-killed animals can become a practice tool, if not too mangled. Please check your game laws to make sure it is legal to possess furbearers (even if picked up as road kill) throughout the year, or whenever you intend to practice.

You'll need some sharp knives, and perhaps a scalpel or two. The topic of a proper skinning knife could occupy the major part of a book, but I'll do my best to it explain briefly, as the final decision is highly subjective. Between my son and me, we've had a few knives that have fit the bill rather well. These include a Puma folding knife with a three and three-quarter-inch clip blade; a Schrade Sharpfinger fixed blade; an Uncle Henry small folding knife (that knife held an edge very well and was perfect for detailed work): and a BladeTech PH Magnum. In addition, I keep a couple scalpels and a couple of knife sharpeners to keep things sharp. My favorite is a folding knife with two slender pointed blades, like the type Blake and Lamb used to make for skinning.

You'll also need a comfortable place to work. It could be on a table in the garage, or on a nail driven in a tree limb out back, used to hang your animal while you skin (I've used both), or any place where you can work undistracted. Indoors is better than outdoors, as it is warmer, and can be utilized in all types of weather and any time of day or night. I've found that a garbage can with a lid and a thick garbage bag liner, along with some really good insect killer, may make life easier, as many of the furbearers play host to fleas, ticks, and other nasty insects. Spray the insect killer in the garbage can, hang the animal in the can by putting a stick or trap stake across the top and through one of the animals back hocks, and put the top on, giving some time to let the creepy-crawly things meet their untimely demise. It acts like a mini gas chamber. It is so much more pleasant and easier to skin a valuable fox, coyote, raccoon, or mink without being bitten by ticks and fleas.

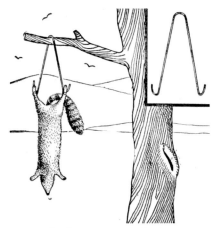

A simple skinning gambrel.

There are two methods of skinning a furbearer. The first, and less popular, is called open-skinned, where the animal is cut in a straight line up the belly from anus to chin, and then skinned as a flat skin. The skin will lay flat on a table, with the spine making the centerline of the skin. This technique is reserved for beaver, badger, and wolverine, as well as for the famous bear skin rug.

Open Skinning (example — beaver)

As with all pelts, before removal they should be clean, dry, and free of all lumps of dirt, blood, and burrs. Place the beaver on its back, with its belly facing upward. Next, using your hand, smooth the fur from the tip of the chin all the way down to the anus. I next take my wetted finger and make a straight fur-row from the chin to the anus. This will be your guide line; if not straight, redo it. Starting at the tail, cut along the line you just made, just under the skin, no deeper, all the way up to the chin. With a beaver you have to be careful not to cut too deeply and into the castors. Next I ring all four feet and the tail at the fur line. Starting with one side of the beaver, in the middle of the belly, grab the fur and pull upward. With your knife cut the material holding the hide to the carcass as you pull the hide. Take special care around the castors, as they are valuable and can sell them or use them yourself in many ways. When you have completed as much as practically can be skinned, turn the beaver and continue the process. Take your time around the eyes, ears, and nose. These are connected to the head with a cartridge-like tissue.

Always cut farther away from the hide and closer to the carcass than you instinctively want to around the head of any animal. Remember 50 percent of skinning an animal is done with your hands. Writing instructions about skinning an animal is a little like writing instruction on telling someone how to swim, to a person that has never done it before. I cannot stress this enough: Try to find a veteran trapper and ask him to show you how to skin any and every animal you intend to trap. Then have him observe your attempting to skin the same animal yourself. You can read ten books on skinning, and watch fifty videos on the topic on YouTube, but it will not come close of what skill you would learn and retain from working with a trapper one on one, for an hour. I have found that 99 percent of trappers would be more than glad to show and teach you, including a few tricks of the trade, as all animals are not the same. Skinning an animal is not a race, so take your time. You are looking for quality not quantity, speed comes with experience. As in most things in life, you have to learn to walk before you can run!

Cased

Most of the furbearers will be "cased," meaning that the fur will be removed from the animal in the same fashion that you or I would remove a T-shirt, over your head, and when completed the T-shirt is completely inside out. There will, for the most part, only be one true cut, and the rest will come off like the case of a sausage. The first cut that needs to be made will run from the lower inner ankle of the rear foot, along the inside of the thigh to the anus, and back down to the opposite inner ankle, and a ring is cut around the lower ankle. I then skin a short portion of each hind leg, exposing the Achilles tendons. Then I attach the animal to either a skinning gambrel or just a chain with a snap or hook on the end. The gambrel or chain should hung from above and be able to be adjusted vertically so you are either sitting or standing straight and not bending over while skinning. There will be times when you are skinning for hours, and poor posture will induce fatigue. Next I ring the front feet at the wrists. Remove hide at the fur line with muskrats and opossums. With all the rest, the tail must be split on the underside and the tailbone removed; the tail should be split open right to the tip. This can be done with the aid if a tail splitter and a tail stripper. The hide and fur are then removed from the body, in a pulling motion, in the manner of removing a T-shirt, using your hands as much as a knife. Most animals have different spots that are a little tricky; on most, around the head is difficult.

On raccoons, for instance, there is a spot just aft and between the front legs; it's very easy to cut the hide right there if not handled just right. You will need to pay special attention once you get up to the base of the neck. Another example is fox; its skin is very thin and fragile, unlike a raccoon's. The trick to cleanly skinning any animal is not cutting the fur off the body—for if you come too close to the actual dermis, you'll invariably cut through it—but to cut *behind* the skin/body attachment, using the off-hand to pull downward on the hide and using the blade to cut the membrane holding the skin to the body; and using your fingers as much as possible. Again, ask a veteran trapper to show you; if you don't know one, look up any trappers' clubs, near or far, and ask. If there is not one close to you, a club out of the area probably knows a few trappers that are close to you. Trappers know each other, and I will be willing to bet there are older gentlemen who used to trap in their younger days, that no longer do so. These men are a wealth of information and wisdom; that is how I obtained my first traps. Also ask at any sport shops, especially if they sell trapping gear or buy furs. I have taught numerous youngsters and sometimes their parents how to properly skin an animal. I was happy to do it, and I made a few friends along the way.

Fleshing

Fleshing is the process in which you remove the unwanted fat and flesh from the hide. Before even starting to flesh a hide, you must make sure it is completely dry and thawed out, and that all burrs and lumps of mud or blood have been removed. If hides have been frozen, let them thaw at room temperature and not from the use of concentrated heat, like a stove. Fatty hides like raccoon or opossum should be allowed to cool so the fat stiffens, as that makes it a lot easier to remove. I would not even attempt to flesh a hide without using a "fleshing beam."

When I first started trapping, I was very fortunate to have the use of one available to me, not to mention the instructor who owned it. That was over fifty-five years ago. His name was David W. Miller, of Linlithgo, New York. This man was like a second father to me, and the things he showed and taught me I carry with me and use to this very day. Some beams are arched and some are flat. If you use a dull, curved, draw shave, then your beam would best work if it is curved to the contour of the tool. If you use a hog scraper, then a flat beam would work best. Scrapers can be purchased or you can make them yourself. Whatever you are most comfortable working with is the one to use. Fleshing incorrectly can cut a hole in the hide, or cut the hair roots, which will affect the value of the pelt in a negative way. Usually, pressing down too hard or having a lump in the fur will be the cause of the damage. Place the hide on the beam, fur side in, and smooth it out by hand. Some trappers will remove any fat and flesh from the very bottom and tail first and then the head, before starting to flesh the main part of the hide. I think it is because they want to get the pain in the neck part completed first, before going to the easier part. When fleshing the main part of the hide, I break it up into two- or three-inch-wide imaginary strips. When I have completed fleshing one strip, I rotate the hide and start the strip next to it, overlapping the strips a little to ensure I did not miss anything. Have a few old rags nearby as you will need them rub off loose fat or soak up any excess grease. You will also need them to clean off your scraper from time to time. A small, sharp knife should be handy to use to scrape (not cut) around tight areas like the ears, eyes, and lips. With open-skinned animals like beaver, it is a little difficult to keep them stationary while you flesh the pelt. You can put a short screw, nail, or fence staple in the top end of your fleshing beam. Then you can hook a leg or eye hole over it to hold the hide in place while you flesh it. Foxes, if skinned properly, will have next to nothing to be removed. I have found scraping (not cutting) with a sharp knife only the few spots where needed will give you the best results, as opposed to needlessly fleshing the complete hide.

During the 1970s, we sold 90 percent of our hides to one fur buyer who came around about every two weeks during season. This particular fur buyer would only reduce the price paid to us by one dollar per hide if the hide was not fleshed and dried. He claimed to own a mechanical fleshing machine; he said that it was quicker, and did a better job than we could do by hand. We figured that we could the time we saved not fleshing hides and put it to use harvesting even more fur and be ahead of the game in the end. Plus there was not any risk of damaging the hide by fleshing or from mice and temperature while drying. All he required was that we skinned the animals as usual, then roll them up, fur side out, place them into a plastic bag, and freeze them. At that time we used bread bags that we saved all summer just for this purpose. When we knew he was coming to buy our fur, we would simply take the hides out of the freezer on a Friday to thaw, and sell on Sunday. If you plan to sell your hides to one fur buyer or another, rather than sending them to a fur auction, ask the fur buyer how he would rather buy them. It may save you time and money; it sure does not do any harm to ask.

Drying

Drying hides is done on a "stretcher." I do not know why they are called stretchers, as they really do not

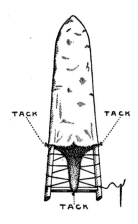

A frame stretcher from yesteryear. Modern stretchers can be totally constructed of wire.

stretch the hide, making it larger than it really is, but rather keep it from shrinking. The more appropriate name would be a fur frame. Stretchers or fur frames are made primarily out of two materials: ones constructed out of wood and ones constructed out of heavy wire.

There are two types in the wood category: a non-adjustable wood board with a separate belly board and an adjustable wooden frame that pivots at the top. The reason for the belly board or the adjustable-type wood frame is that the hide may shrink a little as it dries. You can damage the hide when trying to remove it from a board that does not have a removable belly board to reduce the hide tension, or one that pivots together at the top to make removing the hide easier.

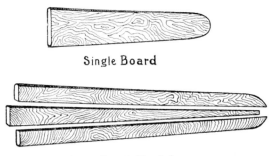

Single Board

Three Board Stretcher

Adjustable and non-adjustable wooden stretchers.

I personally would only use the wire stretchers or frames. Having used both in my life, the wire ones win, hands down. First of all, it takes a fraction of the room to store the wire type rather than wooden ones in off season. As far as price ,they are about the same. The wire type can be cleaned, and will not attract rodents; I cannot say the same for the wooden type. With wire frames, you do not need any push pins or separate belly boards. And secondly, but most important, they make removing the dry hide a breeze, rather than an adventure as do the non-adjustable wooden ones, at times. Most of the time you can tell when a hide has been dried on a wire frame, as opposed to a wood frame; to me the hide dried on a wire frame just looks better. This is especially true with foxes and coyotes, which have to be turned right side out halfway through the drying processes; as they are marketed with the fur side out. When a fox or coyote hide is about half dried—dry enough not to be still sticky, but still pliable and not stiff—it must be turned fur side out, and allowed to complete the drying process.

For all furs with tails, the tails must be pinned open to dry on wood frames or held open on wire stretcher with the claw that is specifically designed for that purpose. Remember, whether using wire or wood, always use the stretcher that fits the hide, rather than try to make the hide fit the stretcher. Drying should be done in a dry, airy, well-ventilated area, with no direct sunlight on the hides. I have at times used a fan to slowly keep the air moving, for fear of mold or mildew. The ideal temperature is about 55°F. It can take between two to five days on average to complete, depending on conditions. Inspect the hides daily, wiping off with a clean rag any excess grease or moisture. When the hides are dry, you can remove them from their frames or stretchers and hang them in a dry area that is rodent free. I will not let my dried hides touch each other, and if hung on a wire or line, I place clothes pins as spacers between them.

Selling Your Fur

There are a few ways to market your fur. One option is a local fur buyer in your area. This is where you take your furs and deal face-to-face with the buyer. He will make comments—both positive and negative—about your fur. You can always learn from these meetings, and improve your fur handling to increase price. You can also ask questions about any comment you do not understand or which you feel is unwarranted. You have the option of accepting the price he or she offers you or rejecting it in hopes of getting a better price elsewhere. Remember, this person needs your furs as much as you want the money for them.

If he does not buy them, he cannot resell them at a profit. Most of the time he will give you a fair price, and if you find out later he did not, lesson learned.

Another option is the traveling or circuit buyer; this is where a buyer comes at timely intervals and buys fur from trappers in the area. He usually meets at a sport shop, gun club, or trappers club. They usually offer the same options as the local buyer, but you at least get to see what he is paying other trappers for comparable fur. You can take his offer, or take your fur back home.

Then there are fur auctions. I have heard good things about fur auctions and I have heard very bad things. Fur auction prices do not only depend on the quality of the fur, but also depend on the ratio of fur to buyers. When there is a lot of fur and few buyers, the prices seem to be weak at best; and adversely, when there are only a few furs and a lot of buyers prices seem to magically rise. If you are there, you can usually buy your own furs back, minus a commission. The other disadvantage is you do not deal with the buyer face to face and never develop a relationship with him.

Mail buyers are a firm that you ship your fur to, and they look at them and give you an offer. In my opinion there are a few drawbacks to this method. One is that you have to box them up and ship them to the buyer; this requires work, time, and money out of pocket. The other problem I have found is once they have your furs, they seem to offer you a generally lower price, preying on the fact that it takes more money to refuse the offer and pay the return shipping. If you choose to decline their offer, you still have to hope to get all your furs back, in as good condition as you sent them, and the correct ones. To me, this is the least positive way to market your hard-earned furs. Options one and two are the best.

Index